SURPRISED BY JOY

BOOKS BY C. S. LEWIS

A Grief Observed
George MacDonald: An Anthology
Mere Christianity
Miracles
The Abolition of Man
The Great Divorce
The Problem of Pain
The Screwtape Letters (with "Screwtape Proposes a Toast")
The Weight of Glory
The Four Loves
Till We Have Faces
Reflections on the Psalms
Letters to Malcolm, Chiefly on Prayer
The Personal Heresy
The World's Last Night: And Other Essays
Poems
The Dark Tower: And Other Stories
Of Other Worlds: Essays and Stories
Narrative Poems
A Mind Awake: An Anthology of C. S. Lewis
Letters of C. S. Lewis
All My Road Before Me
The Business of Heaven: Daily Readings from C. S. Lewis
Present Concerns: Journalistic Essays
Spirits in Bondage: A Cycle of Lyrics
On Stories: And Other Essays on Literature

ALSO AVAILABLE FROM HarperCollins

The Chronicles of Narnia
The Magician's Nephew
The Lion, the Witch and the Wardrobe
The Horse and His Boy
Prince Caspian
The Voyage of the Dawn Treader
The Silver Chair
The Last Battle

SURPRISED BY JOY

THE SHAPE OF MY EARLY LIFE

C. S. Lewis

HarperOne
An Imprint of HarperCollinsPublishers

HarperCollins books may be purchased for educational, business, or sales promotional use. For information, please email the Special Markets Department at SPsales@harpercollins.com.

Originally published in the United Kingdom in 1955 by Geoffrey Bles.

FIRST EDITION

Library of Congress Cataloging-in-Publication Data

Names: Lewis, C. S. (Clive Staples), 1898-1963, author.
Title: Surprised by joy : the shape of my early life / C.S. Lewis.
Description: First edition. | San Francisco : HarperOne, 2017. | Originally published as Surprised by Joy in the United Kingdom in 1955 by Geoffrey Bles.
Identifiers: LCCN 2016030652 | ISBN 9780062565433 (paperback) | ISBN 9780062565440 (e-book)
Subjects: LCSH: Lewis, C. S. (Clive Staples), 1898-1963—Childhood and youth. | Authors, English—20th century—Biography. | Anglican converts—England—Biography. | Christian biography—England. | BISAC: BIOGRAPHY & AUTOBIOGRAPHY / Religious. | RELIGION / Spirituality. | RELIGION / Christianity / Literature & the Arts.
Classification: LCC BV4935.L43 A3 2017 | DDC 248.2/46092 [B]—dc23
LC record available at https://lccn.loc.gov/2016030652

23 24 25 26 27 LBC 18 17 16 15 14

To
Dom Bede Griffiths, O.S.B.

Surprised by joy—impatient as the wind

WORDSWORTH

CONTENTS

PREFACE

This book is written partly in answer to requests that I would tell how I passed from Atheism to Christianity and partly to correct one or two false notions that seem to have got about. How far the story matters to anyone but myself depends on the degree to which others have experienced what I call 'joy'. If it is at all common, a more detailed treatment of it than has (I believe) been attempted before may be of some use. I have been emboldened to write of it because I notice that a man seldom mentions what he had supposed to be his most idiosyncratic sensations without receiving from at least one (often more) of those present the reply, 'What! Have *you* felt that too? I always thought I was the only one.'

The book aims at telling the story of my conversion and is not a general autobiography, still less 'Confessions' like those of St Augustine or Rousseau. This means in practice that it gets less like a general autobiography as it goes on. In the earlier chapters the net has to be spread pretty wide in order that, when the explicitly spiritual crisis arrives, the reader may understand what sort of person my childhood and adolescence had made me. When the 'build-up' is complete, I confine myself strictly to business and omit everything (however important by ordinary biographical standards) which seems, at that stage, irrelevant. I do not think there is much loss; I never read an autobiography in which the parts devoted to the earlier years were not far the most interesting.

The story is, I fear, suffocatingly subjective; the kind of thing I have never written before and shall probably never write again. I have tried so to write the first chapter that those who can't bear such a story will see at once what they are in for and close the book with the least waste of time.

C.S.L.

I

THE FIRST YEARS

Happy, but for so happy ill secured.

MILTON

I was born in the winter of 1898 at Belfast, the son of a solicitor and of a clergyman's daughter. My parents had only two children, both sons, and I was the younger by about three years. Two very different strains had gone to our making. My father belonged to the first generation of his family that reached professional station. His grandfather had been a Welsh farmer; his father, a self-made man, had begun life as a workman, emigrated to Ireland, and ended as a partner in the firm of Macilwaine and Lewis, 'Boiler-makers, Engineers, and Iron Ship Builders'. My mother was a Hamilton with many generations of clergymen, lawyers, sailors, and the like behind her; on her mother's side, through the Warrens, the blood went back to a Norman knight whose bones lie at Battle Abbey. The two families from which I spring were as different in temperament as in origin. My father's people were true Welshmen, sentimental, passionate, and rhetorical, easily moved both to anger and to tenderness; men who laughed and cried a great deal and who had not much of the talent for happiness. The Hamiltons were a cooler race. Their minds were critical and ironic and they had the talent for happiness in a high degree—went straight for it as experienced travellers go for the best seat in a train. From my earliest years I was aware of the vivid contrast between my mother's cheerful and tranquil affection and the ups and downs of my father's emotional life, and this bred in me long before I was old enough to give it a name a certain distrust or dislike of emotion as something uncomfortable and embarrassing and even dangerous.

Both my parents, by the standards of that time and place, were bookish or 'clever' people. My mother had been a promising mathematician in her youth and a BA of Queen's College, Belfast, and before her death was able to start me both in French and Latin. She was a voracious reader of good novels, and I think the Merediths and Tolstoys which I have inherited were bought for her. My father's tastes were quite different. He was fond of oratory and had himself spoken on political platforms in England as a young man; if he had had independent means he would certainly have aimed at a political career. In this, unless his sense of honour, which was fine to the point of being Quixotic, had made him unmanageable, he might well have succeeded, for he had many of the gifts once needed by a Parliamentarian—a fine presence, a resonant voice, great quickness of mind, eloquence, and memory. Trollope's political novels were very dear to him; in following the career of Phineas Finn he was, as I now suppose, vicariously gratifying his own desires. He was fond of poetry provided it had elements of rhetoric or pathos, or both; I think *Othello* was his favourite Shakespearian play. He greatly enjoyed nearly all humorous authors, from Dickens to W. W. Jacobs, and was himself, almost without rival, the best *raconteur* I have ever heard; the best, that is, of his own type, the type that acts all the characters in turn with a free use of grimace, gesture, and pantomime. He was never happier than when closeted for an hour or so with one or two of my uncles exchanging 'wheezes' (as anecdotes were oddly called in our family). What neither he nor my mother had the least taste for was that kind of literature to which my allegiance was given the moment I could choose books for myself. Neither had ever listened for the horns of elfland. There was no copy either of Keats or Shelley in the house, and the copy of Coleridge was never (to my knowledge) opened. If I am a romantic my parents bear no responsibility for it. Tennyson, indeed, my father liked, but it was the Tennyson of *In Memoriam* and *Locksley Hall*. I never heard from him of the *Lotus Eaters* or the *Le Morte d'Arthur*. My mother, I have been told, cared for no poetry at all.

In addition to good parents, good food, and a garden (which then seemed large) to play in, I began life with two other blessings. One was our nurse, Lizzie Endicott, in whom even the exacting memory of childhood can discover no flaw—nothing but kindness, gaiety, and good sense. There was no nonsense about 'lady nurses' in those days. Through Lizzie we struck our roots into the peasantry of County Down. We were thus free of two very different social worlds. To this I owe my lifelong immunity from the false identification which some people make of refinement with virtue. From before I can remember I had understood that certain jokes could be shared with Lizzie which were impossible in the drawing-room; and also that Lizzie was, as nearly as a human can be, simply good.

The other blessing was my brother. Though three years my senior, he never seemed to be an elder brother; we were allies, not to say confederates, from the first. Yet we were very different. Our earliest pictures (and I can remember no time when we were not incessantly drawing) reveal it. His were of ships and trains and battles; mine, when not imitated from his, were of what we both called 'dressed animals'—the anthropomorphised beasts of nursery literature. His earliest story—as my elder he preceded me in the transition from drawing to writing— was called *The Young Rajah*. He had already made India 'his country'; Animal-Land was mine. I do not think any of the surviving drawings date from the first six years of my life which I am now describing, but I have plenty of them that cannot be much later. From them it appears to me that I had the better talent. From a very early age I could draw movement—figures that looked as if they were really running or fighting—and the perspective is good. But nowhere, either in my brother's work or my own, is there a single line drawn in obedience to an idea, how- ever crude, of beauty. There is action, comedy, invention; but there is not even the germ of a feeling for design, and there is a shocking ignorance of natural form. Trees appear as balls of cotton wool stuck on posts, and there is noth- ing to show that either of us knew the shape of any leaf in the garden where we played almost daily. This absence of beauty, now that I come to think of it, is characteristic of our childhood. No picture on the walls of my father's house ever attracted—and indeed none deserved—our attention. We never saw a beautiful building nor imagined that a building could be beautiful. My earliest aesthetic experiences, if indeed they were aesthetic, were not of that kind; they were already incurably romantic, not formal. Once in those very early days my brother brought into the nursery the lid of a biscuit tin which he had covered with moss and garnished with twigs and flowers so as to make it a toy garden or a toy forest. That was the first beauty I ever knew. What the real garden had failed to do, the toy garden did. It made me aware of nature—not, indeed, as a storehouse of forms and colours but as something cool, dewy, fresh, exuberant. I do not think the impression was very important at the moment, but it soon became important in memory. As long as I live my imagination of Paradise will retain something of my brother's toy garden. And every day there were what we called 'the Green Hills'; that is, the low line of the Castlereagh Hills which we saw from the nursery windows. They were not very far off but they were, to children, quite unattainable. They taught me longing—*Sehnsucht;* made me for good or ill, and before I was six years old, a votary of the Blue Flower.

If aesthetic experiences were rare, religious experiences did not occur at all. Some people have got the impression from my books that I was brought up in strict and vivid Puritanism, but this is quite untrue. I was taught the usual things and made to say my prayers and in due time taken to church. I naturally accepted what I was told but I cannot remember feeling much interest in it. My father, far from being specially Puritanical, was, by nineteenth-century and Church of Ireland standards, rather 'high', and his approach to religion, as to literature, was at the opposite pole from what later became my own. The charm of tradition and the verbal beauty of Bible and Prayer Book (all of them for me late and acquired tastes) were his natural delight, and it would have been hard to find an equally intelligent man who cared so little for metaphysics. Of my mother's religion I can say almost nothing from my own memory. My childhood, at all events, was not in the least other-worldly. Except for the toy garden and the Green Hills it was not even imaginative; it lives in my memory mainly as a period of humdrum, prosaic happiness and awakes none of the poignant nostalgia with which I look back on my much less happy boyhood. It is not settled happiness but momentary joy that glorifies the past.

To this general happiness there was one exception. I remember nothing earlier than the terror of certain dreams. It is a very common trouble at that age, yet it still seems to me odd that petted and guarded childhood should so often have in it a window opening on what is hardly less than Hell. My bad dreams were of two kinds, those about spectres and those about insects. The second were, beyond comparison, the worse; to this day I would rather meet a ghost than a tarantula. And to this day I could almost find it in my heart to rationalise and justify my phobia. As Owen Barfield once said to me, 'The trouble about insects is that they are like French locomotives—they have all the works on the outside.' *The works*—that is the trouble. Their angular limbs, their jerky movements, their dry, metallic noises, all suggest either machines that have come to life or life degenerating into mechanism. You may add that in the hive and the ant-hill we see fully realised the two things that some of us most dread for our own species—the dominance of the female and the dominance of the collective. One fact about the history of this phobia is perhaps worth recording. Much later, in my teens, from reading Lubbock's *Ants, Bees and Wasps,* I developed for a short time a genuinely scientific interest in insects. Other studies soon crowded it out; but while my entomological period lasted my fear almost vanished, and I am inclined to think a real objective curiosity will usually have this cleansing effect.

I am afraid the psychologists will not be content to explain my insect fears by what a simpler generation would diagnose as their cause—a certain detestable picture in one of my nursery books. In it a midget child, a sort of Tom Thumb, stood on a toadstool and was threatened from below by a stag-beetle very much larger than himself. This was bad enough; but there is worse to come.

The horns of the beetle were strips of cardboard separate from the plate and working on a pivot. By moving a devilish contraption on the verso you could make them open and shut like pincers: snip-snap—snip-snap—I can see it while I write. How a woman ordinarily so wise as my mother could have allowed this abomination into the nursery is difficult to understand. Unless, indeed (for now a doubt assails me), unless that picture itself is a product of nightmare. But I think not.

In 1905, my seventh year, the first great change in my life took place. We moved house. My father, growing, I suppose, in prosperity, decided to leave the semi-detached villa in which I had been born and built himself a much larger house, further out into what was then the country. The 'New House', as we continued for years to call it, was a large one even by my present standards; to a child it seemed less like a house than a city. My father, who had more capacity for being cheated than any man I have ever known, was badly cheated by his builders; the drains were wrong, the chimneys were wrong, and there was a draught in every room. None of this, however, mattered to a child. To me, the important thing about the move was that the background of my life became larger. The New House is almost a major character in my story. I am a product of long corridors, empty sunlit rooms, upstair indoor silences, attics explored in solitude, distant noises of gurgling cisterns and pipes, and the noise of wind under the tiles. Also, of endless books. My father bought all the books he read and never got rid of any of them. There were books in the study, books in the drawing-room, books in the cloakroom, books (two deep) in the great bookcase on the landing, books in a bedroom, books piled high as my shoulder in the cistern attic, books of all kinds reflecting every transient stage of my parents' interests, books readable and unreadable, books suitable for a child and books most emphatically not. Nothing was forbidden me. In the seemingly endless rainy afternoons I took volume after volume from the shelves. I had always the same certainty of finding a book that was new to me as a man who walks into a field has of finding a new blade of grass. Where all these books had been before we came to the New House is a problem that never occurred to me until I began writing this paragraph. I have no idea of the answer.

Out of doors was 'the view' for which, no doubt, the site had principally been chosen. From our front door we looked down over wide fields to Belfast Lough and across it to the long mountain line of the Antrim shore—Divis, Colin, Cave Hill. This was in the far-off days when Britain was the world's carrier and the Lough was full of shipping; a delight to both us boys, but most to my brother. The sound of a steamer's horn at night still conjures up my whole boyhood. Behind the house, greener, lower, and nearer than the Antrim mountains, were the Holywood Hills, but it was not till much later that they won my attention. The north-western prospect was what mattered at first; the interminable summer sunsets behind the blue ridges, and the rooks flying home. In these surroundings the blows of change began to fall.

First of all, my brother was packed off to an English boarding-school and thus removed from my life for the greater part of every year. I remember well the rapture of his homecomings for the holidays but have no recollection of any corresponding anguish at his departures. His new life made no difference to the relations between us. I, meanwhile, was going on with my education at home; French and Latin from my mother and everything else from an excellent governess, Annie Harper. I made rather a bugbear of this mild and modest little lady at the time, but all that I can remember assures me that I was unjust. She was a Presbyterian; and a longish lecture which she once interpolated between sums and copies is the first thing I can remember that brought the other world to my mind with any sense of reality. But there were many things that I thought about more. My real life—or what memory reports as my real life—was increasingly one of solitude. I had indeed plenty of people to talk to: my parents, my grandfather Lewis, prematurely old and deaf, who lived with us; the maids; and a somewhat bibulous old gardener. I was, I believe, an intolerable chatterbox. But solitude was nearly always at my command, somewhere in the garden or somewhere in the house. I had now learned both to read and write; I had a dozen things to do.

What drove me to write was the extreme manual clumsiness from which I have always suffered. I attribute it to a physical defect which my brother and I both inherit from our father; we have only one joint in the thumb. The upper joint (that farthest from the nail) is visible, but it is a mere sham; we cannot bend it. But whatever the cause, nature laid on me from birth an utter incapacity to make anything. With pencil and pen I was handy enough, and I can still tie as good a bow as ever lay on a man's collar, but with a tool or a bat or a gun, a sleeve-link or a corkscrew, I have always been unteachable. It was this that forced me to write. I longed to make things, ships, houses, engines. Many sheets of cardboard and pairs of scissors I spoiled, only to turn from my hopeless failures in tears. As a last resource, as a *pis aller*, I was driven to write stories instead; little dreaming to what a world of happiness I was being admitted. You can do more with a castle in a story than with the best cardboard castle that ever stood on a nursery table.

I soon staked out a claim to one of the attics and made it 'my study'. Pictures, of my own making or cut from brightly coloured Christmas numbers of magazines, were nailed on the walls. There I kept my pen and inkpot and writing books and paint-box; and there

> *What more felicity can fall to creature*
> *Than to enjoy delight with liberty?*

Here my first stories were written, and illustrated, with enormous satisfaction. They were an attempt to combine my two chief literary pleasures—'dressed animals' and 'knights in armour'. As a result, I wrote about chivalrous mice and rabbits who rode out in complete mail to kill not giants but cats. But already the mood of the systema-tiser was strong in me; the mood which led Trollope so endlessly to elaborate his Barsetshire. The Animal-Land which came into action in the holidays when my brother was at home was a modern Animal-Land; it had to have trains and steamships if it was to be a country shared with him. It followed, of course, that the medieval Animal-Land about which I wrote my stories must be the same country at an earlier period; and of course the two periods must be properly connected. This led me from romanc-ing to historiography; I set about writing a full history of Animal-Land. Though more than one version of this instructive work is extant, I never succeeded in bringing it down to modern times; centuries take a deal of filling when all the events have to come out of the historian's head. But there is one touch in the *History* that I still recall with some pride. The chivalric adventures which filled my stories were in it alluded to very lightly and the reader was warned that they might be 'only legends'. Somehow—but heaven knows how—I realised even then that a historian should adopt a critical attitude towards epic material. From history it was only a step to geography. There was soon a map of Animal-Land—several maps, all tolerably consistent. Then Animal-Land had to be geographically related to my brother's India, and India consequently lifted out of its place in the real world. We made it an island, with its north coast running along the back of the Himalayas; between it and Animal-Land my brother rapidly invented the principal steamship routes. Soon there was a whole world and a map of that world which used every colour in my paint-box. And those parts of that world which we regarded as our own—Animal-Land and India—were increasingly peopled with consistent characters.

Of the books that I read at this time very few have quite faded from memory, but not all have retained my love. Conan Doyle's *Sir Nigel*, which first set my mind upon 'knights in armour', I have never felt inclined to re-read. Still less would I now read Mark Twain's *Yankee at the Court of King Arthur*, which was then my only source for the Arthurian story, blissfully read for the sake of the romantic elements that came through and with total disregard of the vulgar ridicule directed against them. Much better than either of these was E. Nesbit's trilogy, *Five Children and It*, *The Phoenix and the Carpet*, and *The Story of the Amulet*. The last did most for me. It first opened my eyes to antiquity, the 'dark backward and abysm of time'. I can still re-read it with delight. *Gulliver* in an unexpurgated and lavishly illustrated edition was one of my favourites, and I pored endlessly over an almost complete set of old *Punches* which stood in my father's study. Tenniel gratified my passion for 'dressed animals' with his Russian Bear, British Lion, Egyptian Crocodile, and the rest, while his slovenly and perfunctory treatment of vegetation confirmed my own deficiencies. Then came the Beatrix Potter books, and here at last beauty.

It will be clear that at this time—at the age of six, seven, and eight—I was living almost entirely in my imagination; or at least that the imaginative experience of those years now seems to me more important than anything else. Thus I pass over a holiday in Normandy (of which, nevertheless, I retain very clear memories) as a thing of no account; if it could be cut out of my past I should still be almost exactly the man I am. But *imagination* is a vague word and I must make some distinctions. It may mean the world of reverie, day-dream, wish-fulfilling fantasy. Of that I knew more than enough. I often pictured myself cutting a fine figure. But I must insist that this was a totally different activity from the invention of Animal-Land. Animal-Land was not (in that sense) a fantasy at all. I was not one of the characters it contained. I was its creator, not a candidate for admission to it. Invention is essentially different from reverie; if some fail to recognise the difference that is because they have not themselves experienced both. Anyone who has will understand me. In my day-dreams I was training myself to be a fool; in mapping and chronicling Animal-Land I was training myself to be a novelist. Note well, a novelist; not a poet. My invented world was full (for me) of interest, bustle, humour, and character; but there was no poetry, even no romance, in it. It was almost astonishingly prosaic.[1] Thus if we use the word *imagination* in a third sense, and the highest sense of all, this invented world was not imagina-

---

[1] For readers of my children's books, the best way of putting this would be to say that Animal-Land had nothing whatever in common with Narnia except the anthropomorphic beasts. Animal-Land, by its whole quality, excluded the least hint of wonder.

tive. But certain other experiences were, and I will now try to record them. The thing has been much better done by Traherne and Wordsworth, but every man must tell his own tale.

The first is itself the memory of a memory. As I stood beside a flowering currant bush on a summer day there suddenly arose in me without warning, and as if from a depth not of years but of centuries, the memory of that earlier morning at the Old House when my brother had brought his toy garden into the nursery. It is difficult to find words strong enough for the sensation which came over me; Milton's 'enormous bliss' of Eden (giving the full, ancient meaning to 'enormous') comes somewhere near it. It was a sensation, of course, of desire; but desire for what? Not, certainly, for a biscuit-tin filled with moss, nor even (though that came into it) for my own past. Ἰουλίανποθῶ² — and before I knew what I desired, the desire itself was gone, the whole glimpse withdrawn, the world turned commonplace again, or only stirred by a longing for the longing that had just ceased. It had taken only a moment of time; and in a certain sense everything else that had ever happened to me was insignificant in comparison.

The second glimpse came through *Squirrel Nutkin;*

---

² Oh, I desire too much.

through it only, though I loved all the Beatrix Potter books. But the rest of them were merely entertaining; it administered the shock, it was a trouble. It troubled me with what I can only describe as the Idea of Autumn. It sounds fantastic to say that one can be enamoured of a season, but that is something like what happened; and, as before, the experience was one of intense desire. And one went back to the book, not to gratify the desire (that was impossible—how can one *possess* Autumn?) but to re-awake it. And in this experience also there was the same surprise and the same sense of incalculable importance. It was something quite different from ordinary life and even from ordinary pleasure; something, as they would now say, 'in another dimension'.

The third glimpse came through poetry. I had become fond of Longfellow's *Saga of King Olaf:* fond of it in a casual, shallow way for its story and its vigorous rhythms. But then, and quite different from such pleasures, and like a voice from far more distant regions, there came a moment when I idly turned the pages of the book and found the unrhymed translation of *Tegner's Drapa* and read

> *I heard a voice that cried,*
> *Balder the beautiful*
> *Is dead, is dead—*

I knew nothing about Balder; but instantly I was uplifted into huge regions of northern sky, I desired with almost sickening intensity something never to be described (except that it is cold, spacious, severe, pale, and remote) and then, as in the other examples, found myself at the very same moment already falling out of that desire and wishing I were back in it.

The reader who finds these three episodes of no interest need read this book no further, for in a sense the central story of my life is about nothing else. For those who are still disposed to proceed I will only underline the quality common to the three experiences; it is that of an unsatis-fied desire which is itself more desirable than any other satisfaction. I call it Joy, which is here a technical term and must be sharply distinguished both from Happiness and from Pleasure. Joy (in my sense) has indeed one charac-teristic, and one only, in common with them; the fact that anyone who has experienced it will want it again. Apart from that, and considered only in its quality, it might almost equally well be called a particular kind of unhap-piness or grief. But then it is a kind we want. I doubt whether anyone who has tasted it would ever, if both were in his power, exchange it for all the pleasures in the world. But then Joy is never in our power and pleasure often is.

I cannot be absolutely sure whether the things I have

just been speaking of happened before or after the great loss which befell our family and to which I must now turn. There came a night when I was ill and crying both with headache and toothache and distressed because my mother did not come to me. That was because she was ill too; and what was odd was that there were several doctors in her room, and voices, and comings and goings all over the house and doors shutting and opening. It seemed to last for hours. And then my father, in tears, came into my room and began to try to convey to my terrified mind things it had never conceived before. It was in fact cancer and followed the usual course; an operation (they operated in the patient's house in those days), an apparent convalescence, a return of the disease, increasing pain, and death. My father never fully recovered from this loss.

Children suffer not (I think) less than their elders, but differently. For us boys the real bereavement had happened before our mother died. We lost her gradually as she was gradually withdrawn from our life into the hands of nurses and delirium and morphia, and as our whole existence changed into something alien and menacing, as the house became full of strange smells and midnight noises and sinister whispered conversations. This had two further results, one very evil and one very good. It divided us from our father as well as our mother. They say that a shared sorrow draws people closer together; I can hardly believe that it often has that effect when those who share it are of widely different ages. If I may trust to my own experience, the sight of adult misery and adult terror has an effect on children which is merely paralysing and alienating. Perhaps it was our fault. Perhaps if we had been better children we might have lightened our father's sufferings at this time. We certainly did not. His nerves had never been of the steadiest and his emotions had always been uncontrolled. Under the pressure of anxiety his temper became incalculable; he spoke wildly and acted unjustly. Thus by a peculiar cruelty of fate, during those months the unfortunate man, had he but known it, was really losing his sons as well as his wife. We were coming, my brother and I, to rely more and more exclusively on each other for all that made life bearable; to have confidence only in each other. I expect that we (or at any rate I) were already learning to lie to him. Everything that had made the house a home had failed us; everything except one another. We drew daily closer together (that was the good result)—two frightened urchins huddled for warmth in a bleak world.

Grief in childhood is complicated with many other miseries. I was taken into the bedroom where my mother lay dead; as they said, 'to see her', in reality, as I at once knew, 'to see it'. There was nothing that a grown-up would call disfigurement—except for that total disfigurement which is death itself. Grief was overwhelmed in terror. To this day I do not know what they mean when they call dead bodies beautiful. The ugliest man alive is an angel of beauty compared with the loveliest of the dead. Against all the subsequent paraphernalia of coffin, flowers, hearse, and funeral I reacted with horror. I even lectured one of my aunts on the absurdity of mourning clothes in a style which would have seemed to most adults both heartless and precocious; but this was our dear Aunt Annie, my maternal uncle's Canadian wife, a woman almost as sensible and sunny as my mother herself. To my hatred for what I already felt to be all the fuss and flummery of the funeral I may perhaps trace something in me which I now recognise as a defect but which I have never fully overcome—a distaste for all that is public, all that belongs to the collective; a boorish inaptitude for formality.

My mother's death was the occasion of what some (but not I) might regard as my first religious experience. When her case was pronounced hopeless I remembered what I had been taught; that prayers offered in faith would be granted. I accordingly set myself to produce by willpower a firm belief that my prayers for her recovery would be successful; and, as I thought, I achieved it. When nevertheless she died I shifted my ground and worked myself into a belief that there was to be a miracle. The interesting thing is that my disappointment produced no results beyond itself. The thing hadn't worked, but I was used to things not working, and I thought no more about it. I think the truth is that the belief into which I had hypnotised myself was itself too irreligious for its failure to cause any religious revolution. I had approached God, or my idea of God, without love, without awe, even without fear. He was, in my mental picture of this miracle, to appear neither as Saviour nor as Judge, but merely as a magician; and when He had done what was required of Him I supposed He would simply—well, go away. It never crossed my mind that the tremendous contact which I solicited should have any consequences beyond restoring the *status quo*. I imagine that a 'faith' of this kind is often generated in children and that its disappointment is of no religious importance; just as the things believed in, if they could happen and be only as the child pictures them, would be of no religious importance either.

With my mother's death all settled happiness, all that was tranquil and reliable, disappeared from my life. There was to be much fun, many pleasures, many stabs of Joy; but no more of the old security. It was sea and islands now; the great continent had sunk like Atlantis.

II

CONCENTRATION CAMP

Arithmetic with Coloured Rods.
>   *Times Educational Supplement,*
>   19 November 1954

Clop-clop-clop-clop . . . we are in a four-wheeler rattling over the uneven squaresets of the Belfast streets through the damp twilight of a September evening, 1908; my father, my brother, and I. I am going to school for the first time. We are in low spirits. My brother, who has most reason to be so, for he alone knows what we are going to, shows his feelings least. He is already a veteran. I perhaps am buoyed up by a little excitement, but very little. The most important fact at the moment is the horrible clothes I have been made to put on. Only this morning—only two hours ago—I was running wild in shorts and blazer and sandshoes. Now I am choking and sweating, itching too, in thick dark stuff, throttled by an Eton collar, my feet already aching with unaccustomed boots. I am wearing knickerbockers that button at the knee. Every night for some forty weeks of every year and for many a year I am to see the red, smarting imprint of those buttons in my flesh when I undress. Worst of all is the bowler-hat, apparently made of iron, which grasps my head. I have read of boys in the same predicament who welcomed such things as signs of growing up; I had no such feeling. Nothing in my experience had ever suggested to me that it was nicer to be a schoolboy than a child or nicer to be a man than a schoolboy. My brother never talked much about school in the holidays. My father, whom I implicitly believed, represented adult life as one of incessant drudgery under the continual threat of financial ruin. In this he did not mean to deceive us. Such was his temperament that when he exclaimed, as he frequently did, 'There'll soon be nothing for it but the workhouse,' he momentarily believed, or at least felt, what he said. I took it all literally and had the gloomiest anticipation of adult life. In the meantime, the putting on of the school clothes was, I well knew, the assumption of a prison uniform.

We reach the quay and go on board the old 'Fleetwood boat'; after some miserable strolling about the deck my father bids us good-bye. He is deeply moved; I, alas, am mainly embarrassed and self-conscious. When he has gone ashore we almost, by comparison, cheer up. My brother begins to show me over the ship and tell me about all the other shipping in sight. He is an experienced traveller and a complete man of the world. A certain agreeable excitement steals over me. I like the reflected port and starboard lights on the oily water, the rattle of winches, the warm smell from the engine-room skylight. We cast off. The black space widens between us and the quay; I feel the throb of screws underneath me. Soon we are dropping down the Lough and there is a taste of salt on one's lips, and that cluster of lights astern, receding from us, is everything I have known. Later, when we have gone to our bunks, it begins to blow. It is a rough night and my brother is sea-sick. I absurdly envy him this accomplishment. He is behaving as experienced travellers should. By great efforts I succeed in vomiting; but it is a poor affair—I was, and am, an obstinately good sailor.

No Englishman will be able to understand my first impressions of England. When we disembarked, I suppose at about six next morning (but it seemed to be midnight), I found myself in a world to which I reacted with immediate hatred. The flats of Lancashire in the early morning are in reality a dismal sight; to me they were like the banks of Styx. The strange English accents with which I was surrounded seemed like the voices of demons. But what was worst was the English landscape from Fleetwood to Euston. Even to my adult eye that main line still appears to run through the dullest and most unfriendly strip in the island. But to a child who had always lived near the sea and in sight of high ridges it appeared as I suppose Russia might appear to an English boy. The flatness! The interminableness! The miles and miles of featureless land, shutting one in from the sea, imprisoning, suffocating! Everything was wrong; wooden fences instead of stone walls and hedges, red brick farmhouses instead of white cottages, the fields too big, haystacks the wrong shape. Well does the *Kalevala* say that in the stranger's house the floor is full of knots. I have made up the quarrel since; but at that moment I conceived a hatred for England which took many years to heal.

Our destination was the little town of—let us call it Belsen—in Hertfordshire. 'Green Hertfordshire', Lamb calls it; but it was not green to a boy bred in County Down. It was flat Hertfordshire, flinty Hertfordshire, Hertfordshire of the yellow soil. There is the same difference between the climate of Ireland and of England as between that of England and the Continent. There was far more weather at Belsen than I had ever met before; there I first knew bitter frost and stinging fog, sweltering heat and thunderstorms on the great scale. There, through the curtainless dormitory windows, I first came to know the ghastly beauty of the full moon.

The school, as I first knew it, consisted of some eight or nine boarders and about as many day-boys. Organised games, except for endless rounders in the flinty play-ground, had long been moribund and were finally abandoned not very long after my arrival. There was no bathing except one's weekly bath in the bathroom. I was already doing Latin exercises (as taught by my mother) when I went there in 1908, and I was still doing Latin exercises when I left there in 1910; I had never got in sight of a Roman author. The only stimulating element in the teaching consisted of a few well-used canes which hung on the green iron chimney-piece of the single schoolroom. The teaching staff consisted of the headmaster and proprietor (we called him Oldie), his grown-up son (Wee Wee), and an usher. The ushers succeeded one another with great rapidity; one lasted for less than a week. Another was dismissed in the presence of the boys, with a rider from Oldie to the effect that if he were not in Holy Orders he would kick him downstairs. This curious scene took place in the dormitory, though I cannot remember why. All these ushers (except the one who stayed less than a week) were obviously as much in awe of Oldie as we. But there came a time when there were no more ushers, and Oldie's youngest daughter taught the junior pupils. By that time there were only five boarders, and Oldie finally gave up his school and sought a cure of souls. I was one of the last survivors, and left the ship only when she went down under us.

Oldie lived in a solitude of power, like a sea-captain in the days of sail. No man or woman in that house spoke to him as an equal. No one except Wee Wee initiated conversation with him at all. At meal times we boys had a glimpse of his family life. His son sat on his right hand; they two had separate food. His wife and three grown-up daughters (silent), the usher (silent), and the boys (silent) munched their inferior messes. His wife, though I think she never addressed Oldie, was allowed to make something of a reply to him; the girls—three tragic figures, dressed summer and winter in the same shabby black—never went beyond an almost whispered 'Yes, Papa,' or 'No, Papa,' on the rare occasions when they were addressed. Few visitors entered the house. Beer, which Oldie and Wee Wee drank regularly at dinner, was offered to the usher but he was expected to refuse; the one who accepted got his pint, but was taught his place by being asked a few moments later in a voice of thunderous irony, 'Perhaps you would like a little *more* beer, Mr N.?' Mr N., a man of spirit, replied casually, 'Well, thank you, Mr C., I think I would.' He was the one who did not stay till the end of his first week; and the rest of that day was a black one for us boys.

I myself was rather a pet or mascot of Oldie's—a position which I swear I never sought and of which the advantages were purely negative. Even my brother was not one of his favourite victims. For he had his favourite victims, boys who could do nothing right. I have known Oldie enter the schoolroom after breakfast, cast his eyes round, and remark, 'Oh, there you are, Rees, you horrid boy. If I'm not too tired I shall give you a good drubbing this afternoon.' He was not angry, nor was he joking. He was a big, bearded man with full lips like an Assyrian king on a monument, immensely strong, physically dirty. Everyone talks of sadism nowadays but I question whether his cruelty had any erotic element in it. I half divined then, and seem to see clearly now, what all his whipping-boys had in common. They were the boys who fell below a certain social status, the boys with vulgar accents. Poor P.—dear, honest, hard-working, friendly, healthily pious P.—was flogged incessantly, I now think, for one offence only; he was the son of a dentist. I have seen Oldie make that child bend down at one end of the schoolroom and then take a run of the room's length at each stroke; but P. was the trained sufferer of countless thrashings and no sound escaped him until, towards the end of the torture, there came a noise quite unlike a human utterance. That peculiar croaking or rattling cry, that, and the grey faces of all the other boys, and their deathlike stillness, are among the memories I could willingly dispense with.[1]

The curious thing is that despite all this cruelty we did surprisingly little work. This may have been partly because the cruelty was irrational and unpredictable; but it was partly because of the curious methods employed. Except at geometry (which he really liked) it might be said that Oldie did not teach at all. He called his class up and asked questions. When the replies were unsatisfactory he said in a low, calm voice, 'Bring me my cane. I see I shall need it.' If a boy became confused Oldie flogged the desk, shouting in a crescendo, 'Think—Think—THINK!!' Then, as the prelude to execution, he muttered, 'Come out, come out, come out.' When really angry he proceeded to antics; worming for wax in his ear with his little finger and babbling, 'Aye, aye, aye, aye . . .' I have seen him leap up and dance round and round like a performing bear. Meanwhile, almost in whispers, Wee Wee or the usher, or (later) Oldie's youngest daughter, was questioning us juniors at another desk. 'Lessons' of this sort did not take very long; what was to be done with the boys for the rest of the time? Oldie had decided that they could, with least trouble to himself, be made to do arithmetic. Accordingly,

---

[1] This punishment was for a mistake in a geometrical proof.

when you entered school at nine o'clock you took your slate and began doing sums. Presently you were called up to 'say a lesson'. When that was finished you went back to your place and did more sums—and so for ever. All the other arts and sciences thus appeared as islands (mostly rocky and dangerous islands)

> *Which like to rich and various gems inlaid*
> *The unadorned bosom of the deep*

—the deep being a shoreless ocean of arithmetic. At the end of the morning you had to say how many sums you had done; and it was not quite safe to lie. But supervision was slack and very little assistance was given. My brother—I have told you that he was already a man of the world—soon found the proper solution. He announced every morning with perfect truth that he had done five sums; he did not add that they were the same five every day. It would be interesting to know how many thousand times he did them.

I must restrain myself. I could continue to describe Oldie for many pages; some of the worst is unsaid. But perhaps it would be wicked, and it is certainly not obligatory, to do so. One good thing I can tell of him. Impelled by conscience, a boy once confessed to him an otherwise undetectable lie. The ogre was touched; he only patted the terrified boy's back and said, 'Always stick to the truth.' I can also say that though he taught geometry cruelly, he taught it well. He forced us to reason, and I have been the better for those geometry lessons all my life. For the rest, there is a possible explanation of his behaviour which renders it more forgivable. Years after, my brother met a man who had grown up in the house next door to Oldie's school. That man and his family, and (I think) the neighbours in general, believed Oldie to be insane. Perhaps they were right. And if he had fairly recently become so, it would explain a thing which puzzles me. At that school as I knew it most boys learned nothing and no boy learned much. But Oldie could boast an impressive record of scholarships in the past. His school cannot always have been the swindle it was in our time.

You may ask how our father came to send us there. Certainly not because he made a careless choice. The surviving correspondence shows that he had considered many other schools before fixing on Oldie's; and I know him well enough to be sure that in such a matter he would never have been guided by his first thoughts (which would probably have been right) nor even by his twenty-first (which would at least have been explicable). Beyond doubt he would have prolonged deliberation till his hundred-and-first; and they would be infallibly and invincibly wrong. This is what always happens to the deliberations of a simple man who thinks he is a subtle one. Like Earle's *Scepticke in Religion* he 'is alwayes too hard for himself'. My father piqued himself on what he called 'reading between the lines'. The obvious meaning of any fact or document was always suspect: the true and inner meaning, invisible to all eyes except his own, was unconsciously created by the restless fertility of his imagination. While he thought he was interpreting Oldie's prospectus, he was really composing a school story in his own mind. And all this, I doubt not, with extreme conscientiousness and even some anguish. It might, perhaps, have been expected that this story of his would presently be blown away by the real story which we had to tell after we had gone to Belsen. But this did not happen. I believe it rarely happens. If the parents in each generation always or often knew what really goes on at their sons' schools, the history of education would be very different. At any rate, my brother and I certainly did not succeed in impressing the truth on our father's mind. For one thing (and this will become clearer in the sequel) he was a man not easily informed. His mind was too active to be an accurate receiver. What he thought he had heard was never exactly what you had said. We did not even try very hard. Like other children, we had no standard of comparison; we supposed the miseries of Belsen to be the common and unavoidable miseries of all schools. Vanity helped to tie our tongues. A boy home from school (especially during that first week when the holidays seem eternal) likes to cut a dash. He would rather represent his master as a buffoon than an ogre. He would hate to be thought a coward and a cry-baby, and he cannot paint the true picture of his concentration camp without admitting himself to have been for the last thirteen weeks a pale, quivering, tear-stained, obsequious slave. We all like showing scars received in battle; the wounds of the *ergastulum,* less. My father must not bear the blame for our wasted and miserable years at Oldie's; and now, in Dante's words, 'to treat of the good that I found there'.

First, I learned, if not friendship, at least gregariousness. There had been bullying at the school when my brother first went there. I had my brother's protection for my first few terms (after which he left to go to a school we may call Wyvern) but I doubt if it was necessary. During those last declining years of the school we boarders were too few and too badly treated to do or suffer much in that way. Also, after a certain time, there were no new boys. We had our quarrels, which seemed serious enough at the time; but long before the end we had known one another too long and suffered too much together not to be, at the least, very old acquaintance. That, I think, is why Belsen did me, in the long run, so little harm. Hardly any amount of oppression from above takes the heart out of a boy like oppression from his fellows. We had many pleasant hours alone together, we five remaining boarders. The abandonment of organised games, though a wretched preparation for the public school life to which most of us were destined, was at the time a great blessing. We were sent out for walks alone on half holidays. We did not do much walking. We bought sweets in drowsy village shops and pottered about on the canal bank or sat at the brow of a railway cutting watching a tunnel-mouth for trains. Hertfordshire came to look less hostile. Our talk was not bound down to the narrow interests which satisfy public school boys; we still had the curiosity of children. I can even remember from those days what must have been the first metaphysical argument I ever took part in. We debated whether the future was like a line you can't see or like a line that is not yet drawn. I have forgotten which side I took though I know that I took it with great zeal. And always there was what Chesterton calls 'the slow maturing of old jokes'.

The reader will notice that school was thus coming to reflect a pattern I had already encountered in my home life. At home, the bad times had drawn my brother and me closer together; here, where the times were always bad, the fear and hatred of Oldie had something of the same effect upon us all. His school was in some ways very like Dr Grimstone's school in *Vice Versa;* but unlike Dr Grimstone's it contained no informer. We stood four-square against the common enemy. I suspect that this pattern, occurring twice and so early in my life, has unduly biassed my whole outlook. To this day the vision of the world which comes most naturally to me is one in which 'we two' or 'we few' (and in a sense 'we happy few') stand together against something stronger and larger. England's position in 1940 was to me no surprise; it was the sort of thing that I always expect. Hence while friendship has been by far the chief source of my happiness, acquaintance or general society has always meant little to me, and I cannot quite understand why a man should wish to know more people than he can make real friends of. Hence, too, a very defective, perhaps culpably defective, interest in large impersonal movements, causes and the like. The concern aroused in me by a battle (whether in story or in reality) is almost in an inverse ratio to the number of the combatants.

In another way too Oldie's school presently repeated my home experience. Oldie's wife died; and in term time.

He reacted to bereavement by becoming more violent than before; so much so that Wee Wee made a kind of apology for him to the boys. You will remember that I had already learned to fear and hate emotion; here was a fresh reason to do so.

But I have not yet mentioned the most important thing that befell me at Oldie's. There first I became an effective believer. As far as I know, the instrument was the church to which we were taken twice every Sunday. This was high 'Anglo-Catholic'. On the conscious level I reacted strongly against its peculiarities—was I not an Ulster Protestant, and were not these unfamiliar rituals an essential part of the hated English atmosphere? Unconsciously, I suspect, the candles and incense, the vestments and the hymns sung on our knees, may have had a considerable, and opposite, effect on me. But I do not think they were the important thing. What really mattered was that I here heard the doctrines of Christianity (as distinct from general 'uplift') taught by men who obviously believed them. As I had no scepticism, the effect was to bring to life what I would already have said that I believed. In this experience there was a great deal of fear. I do not think there was more than was wholesome or even necessary; but if in my books I have spoken too much of Hell, and if critics want a historical explanation of the fact, they must seek it not in the supposed Puritanism of my Ulster childhood but in the Anglo-Catholicism of the church at Belsen. I feared for my soul; especially on certain blazing moonlight nights in that curtainless dormitory—how the sound of other boys breathing in their sleep comes back! The effect, so far as I can judge, was entirely good. I began seriously to pray and to read my Bible and to attempt to obey my conscience. Religion was among the subjects which we often discussed; discussed, if my memory serves me, in an entirely healthy and profitable way, with great gravity and without hysteria, and without the shamefacedness of older boys. How I went back from this beginning you shall hear later.

Intellectually, the time I spent at Oldie's was almost entirely wasted; if the school had not died, and if I had been left there two years more, it would probably have sealed my fate as a scholar for good. Geometry and some pages in *West's English Grammar* (but even those I think I found for myself) are the only items on the credit side. For the rest, all that rises out of the sea of arithmetic is a jungle of dates, battles, exports, imports, and the like, forgotten as soon as learned and perfectly useless had they been remembered. There was also a great decline in my imaginative life. For many years Joy (as I have defined it) was not only absent but forgotten. My reading was now mainly rubbish; but as there was no library at the school we must not make Oldie responsible for that. I read twaddling school stories in *The Captain*. The pleasure here was, in the proper sense, mere wish-fulfilment and fantasy; one enjoyed vicariously the triumphs of the hero. When the boy passes from nursery literature to school-stories he is going down, not up. *Peter Rabbit* pleases a disinterested imagination, for the child does not want to be a rabbit, though he may like pretending to be a rabbit as he may later like acting Hamlet; but the story of the unpromising boy who became captain of the First Eleven exists precisely to feed his real ambitions. I also developed a great taste for all the fiction I could get about the ancient world: *Quo Vadis, Darkness and Dawn, The Gladiators, Ben Hur.* It might be expected that this arose out of my new concern for my religion, but I think not. Early Christians came into many of these stories, but they were not what I was after. I simply wanted sandals, temples, togas, slaves, emperors, galleys, amphitheatres; the attraction, as I now see, was erotic, and erotic in rather a morbid way. And they were mostly, as literature, rather bad books. What has worn better, and what I took to at the same time, is the work of Rider Haggard; and also the 'scientifiction' of H. G. Wells. The idea of other planets exercised upon me then a peculiar, heady attraction, which was quite different from any other of my literary interests. Most emphatically it was not the romantic spell of *Das Ferne*. 'Joy' (in my technical sense) never darted from Mars or the Moon. This was something coarser and stronger. The interest, when the fit was upon me, was ravenous, like a lust. This particular coarse strength I have come to accept as a mark that the interest which has it is psychological, not spiritual; behind such a fierce tang there lurks, I suspect, a psychoanalytical explanation. I may perhaps add that my own planetary romances have been not so much the gratification of that fierce curiosity as its exorcism. The exorcism worked by reconciling it with, or subjecting it to, the other, the more elusive, and genuinely imaginative, impulse. That the ordinary interest in scientifiction is an affair for psychoanalysts is borne out by the fact that all who like it, like it thus ravenously, and equally by the fact that those who do not, are often nauseated by it. The repulsion of the one sort has the same coarse strength as the fascinated interest of the other and is equally a tell-tale.

So much for Oldie's; but the year was not all term. Life at a vile boarding-school is in this way a good preparation for the Christian life, that it teaches one to live by hope. Even, in a sense, by faith, for at the beginning of each term, home and the holidays are so far off that it is

as hard to realise them as to realise heaven. They have
the same pitiful unreality when confronted with immediate horrors. To-morrow's geometry blots out the distant
end of term as to-morrow's operation may blot out the
hope of Paradise. And yet, term after term, the unbelievable happened. Fantastical and astronomical figures like
'This time six weeks' shrank into practicable figures like
'This time next week', and then 'This time to-morrow',
and the almost supernatural bliss of the Last Day punctu-
ally appeared. It was a delight that almost demanded to be
stayed with flagons and comforted with apples; a delight
that tingled down the spine and troubled the belly and
at moments went near to stopping the breath. Of course
this had a terrible and equally relevant reverse side. In
the first week of the holidays we might acknowledge that
term would come again—as a young man in peace-time,
in full health, acknowledges that he will one day die. But
like him we could not even by the grimmest *memento
mori* be brought to realise it. And there too, each time, the
unbelievable happened. The grinning skull finally peered
through all disguises; the last hour, held at bay by every
device our will and imaginations knew, came in the end,
and once more it was the bowler-hat, the Eton collar, the
knickerbockers, and (clop-clop-clop-clop) the evening
drive to the quay. In all seriousness I think that the life of

faith is easier to me because of these memories. To think, in sunny and confident times, that I shall die and rot, or to think that one day all this universe will slip away and become memory (as Oldie slipped away into memory three times a year, and with him the canes and the disgusting food, the stinking sanitation and the cold beds)—this is easier to us if we have seen just that sort of thing happening before. We have learned not to take present things at their face value.

In attempting to give an account of our home life at this time I am troubled by doubts about chronology. School affairs can to some extent be dated by surviving records, but the slow, continuous unfolding of family life escapes them. Our slight alienation from our father imperceptibly increased. In part no one was to blame; in a very great part we were to blame. A temperamental widower, still prostrated by the loss of his wife, must be a very good and wise man indeed if he makes no mistakes in bringing up two noisy and mischievous schoolboys who reserve their confidence wholly for each other. And my father's good qualities as well as his weaknesses incapacitated him for the task. He was far too manly and generous to strike a child for the gratification of his anger; and he was too impulsive ever to punish a child in cold blood and on principle. He therefore relied wholly on his tongue as the instrument of domestic discipline. And here that fatal bent towards dramatisation and rhetoric (I speak of it the more freely since I inherit it) produced a pathetic yet comic result. When he opened his mouth to reprove us he no doubt intended a short well-chosen appeal to our common sense and conscience. But alas, he had been a public speaker long before he became a father. He had for many years been a public prosecutor. Words came to him and intoxicated him as they came. What actually happened was that a small boy who had walked on damp grass in his slippers or left a bathroom in a pickle found himself attacked with something like Cicero on Catiline or Burke on Warren Hastings; simile piled on simile, rhetorical question on rhetorical question, the flash of an orator's eye and the thundercloud of an orator's brow, the gestures, the cadences, and the pauses. The pauses might be the chief danger. One was so long that my brother, quite innocently supposing the denunciation to have ended, humbly took up his book and resumed his reading; a gesture which my father (who had after all only made a rhetorical miscalculation of about a second and a half) not unnaturally took for 'cool, premeditated insolence'. The ludicrous disproportion between such harangues and their occasions puts me in mind of the advocate in Martial who thunders about all the villains of Roman history while meantime *lis est de tribus capellis*—

This case, I beg the court to note,
Concerns a trespass by a goat.

My poor father, while he spoke, forgot not only the offence, but the capacities, of his audience. All the resources of his immense vocabulary were poured forth. I can still remember such words as *abominable, sophisticated,* and *surreptitious.* You will not get the full flavour unless you know an angry Irishman's energy in explosive consonants and the rich growl of his R's. A worse treatment could hardly have been applied. Up to a certain age these invectives filled me with boundless terror and dismay. From the wilderness of the adjectives and the welter of the unintelligible, emerged ideas which I thought I understood only too well, as I heard with implicit and literal belief that our father's ruin was approaching, that we should all soon beg our bread in the streets, that he would shut up the house and keep us at school all the year round, that we should be sent to the colonies and there end in misery the career of crime on which we had, it seemed, already embarked. All security seemed to be taken from me; there was no solid ground beneath my feet. It is significant that at this time if I woke in the night and did not immediately hear my brother's breathing from the neighbouring bed, I often suspected that my father and he had secretly risen while

I slept and gone off to America—that I was finally abandoned. Such was the effect of my father's rhetoric up to
a certain age; then, quite suddenly, it became ridiculous.
I can even remember the moment of the change, and the
story well illustrates both the justice of my father's anger
and the unhappy way in which he expressed it. One day
my brother decided it would be a good thing to make a
tent. Accordingly we procured a dust-sheet from one of
the attics. The next step was to find uprights; the step-
ladder in the wash-house suggested itself. For a boy with
a hatchet it was the work of a moment to reduce this to
a number of disconnected poles. Four of these were then
planted in the earth and the sheet draped over them. To
make sure that the whole structure was really reliable my
brother then tried sitting on the top of it. We remembered
to put away the ragged remains of the sheet but quite forgot about the uprights. That evening, when my father had
come home from work and dined, he went for a stroll in
the garden, accompanied by us. The sight of four slender
wooden posts rising from the grass moved in him a par-
donable curiosity. Interrogation followed; on this occasion we told the truth. Then the lightnings flashed and
the thunder roared; and all would have gone now as it had
gone on a dozen previous occasions, but for the climax—
'Instead of which I find you have cut up the step-ladder.

And what for, forsooth? To make a thing like an abortive Punch-and-Judy show.' At that moment we both hid our faces; not, alas, to cry.

As will be seen from this anecdote one dominant factor in our life at home was the daily absence of our father from about nine in the morning till six at night. For the rest of the day we had the house to ourselves, except for the cook and housemaid with whom we were sometimes at war and sometimes in alliance. Everything invited us to develop a life that had no connection with our father. The most important of our activities was the endless drama of Animal-Land and India, and this of itself isolated us from him.

But I must not leave the reader under the impression that all the happy hours of the holidays occurred during our father's absence. His temperament was mercurial, his spirits rose as easily as they fell, and his forgiveness was as thorough-going as his displeasure. He was often the most jovial and companionable of parents. He could 'play the fool' as well as any of us, and had no regard for his own dignity, 'conned no state'. I could not, of course, at that age see what good company (by adult standards) he was, his humour being of the sort that requires at least some knowledge of life for its full appreciation; I merely basked in it as in fine weather. And all the time there was the sen-

suous delight of being at home, the delight of luxury—
'civilisation', as we called it. I spoke just now of *Vice
Versa*. Its popularity was surely due to something more
than farce. It is the only truthful school story in existence. The machinery of the Garuda Stone really serves
to bring out in their true colours (which would otherwise
seem exaggerated) the sensations which every boy had on
passing from the warmth and softness and dignity of his
home life to the privations, the raw and sordid ugliness, of
school. I say 'had' not 'has'; for perhaps homes have gone
down in the world and schools gone up since then.

It will be asked whether we had no friends, no neighbours, no relatives. We had. To one family in particular
our debt is so great that it had better be left, with some
other matters, to the next chapter.

III

MOUNTBRACKEN AND CAMPBELL

For all these fair people in the hall were in their first
age; none happier under the heaven; their king, the
man of noblest temper. It would be a hard task
to-day to find so brave a fellowship in any castle.

Gawain and the Green Knight

To speak of my nearer relatives is to remind myself how
the contrast of Lewis and Hamilton dominated my whole
early life. It began, for me, with the grandparents. Grandfather Lewis, deaf, slow-moving, humming his psalm
chants, much concerned for his health and prone to remind the family that he would not be with them long, is
contrasted with Grandmother Hamilton, the sharp-
tongued, sharp-witted widow, full of heterodox opinions
(even, to the scandal of the whole connection, a Home
Ruler), every inch a Warren, indifferent to convention as
only an old Southern Irish aristocrat could be, living alone
in a large tumble-down house with half a hundred cats for

company. To how many an innocent conversational gambit did she reply, 'You're talking great nonsense'? Born a little later, she would, I think, have been a Fabian. She met vague small talk with ruthless statements of ascertainable fact and well-worn maxims with a tart demand for evidence. Naturally, people called her eccentric. Coming down a generation I find the same opposition. My father's elder brother 'Uncle Joe', with his family of two boys and three girls, lived very close to us while we were at the Old House. His younger son was my earliest friend, but we drifted apart as we grew older. Uncle Joe was both a clever man and a kind, and especially fond of me. But I remember nothing that was said by our elders in that house; it was simply 'grown-up' conversation—about people, business, politics, and health, I suppose. But 'Uncle Gussie'—my mother's brother, A. W. Hamilton—talked to me as if we were of an age. That is, he talked about Things. He told me all the science I could then take in, clearly, eagerly, without silly jokes and condescensions, obviously liking it as much as I did. He thus provided the intellectual background for my reading of H. G. Wells. I do not suppose he cared for me as a person half so much as Uncle Joe did; and that (call it an injustice or not) was what I liked. During these talks our attention was fixed not on one another but on the subject. His Canadian wife I have already mentioned. In her also I found what I liked best—an unfailing, kindly welcome without a hint of sentimentality, unruffled good sense, the unobtrusive talent for making all things at all times as cheerful and comfortable as circumstances allowed. What one could not have one did without and made the best of it. The tendency of the Lewises to re-open wounds and to rouse sleeping dogs was unknown to her as to her husband.

But we had other kin who mattered to us far more than our aunts and uncles. Less than a mile from our home stood the largest house I then knew, which I will here call Mountbracken, and there lived Sir W. E. Lady E. was my mother's first cousin and perhaps my mother's dearest friend, and it was no doubt for my mother's sake that she took upon herself the heroic work of civilising my brother and me. We had a standing invitation to lunch at Mountbracken whenever we were at home; to this, almost entirely, we owe it that we did not grow up savages. The debt is not only to Lady E. ('Cousin Mary') but to her whole family; walks, motor-drives (in those days an exciting novelty), picnics, and invitations to the theatre were showered on us, year after year, with a kindness which our rawness, our noise, and our unpunctuality never seemed to weary. We were at home there almost as much as in our own house, but with this great difference, that a certain standard of manners had to be kept up. Whatever I know (it is not much) of courtesy and *savoir faire* I learned at Mountbracken.

Sir W. ('Cousin Quartus') was the eldest of several brothers who owned between them one of the most important industrial concerns in Belfast. He belonged in fact to just that class and generation of which the modern man gets his impressions through Galsworthy's Forsytes. Unless Cousin Quartus was very untrue to type (he may well have been) that impression is grossly unjust. No one less like a Galsworthian character ever existed. He was gracious, childlike, deeply and religiously humble, and abounding in charity. No man could feel more fully his responsibility to dependants. He had a good deal of boy-ish gaiety about him; at the same time I always felt that the conception of duty dominated his life. His stately figure, his grey beard, and his strikingly handsome pro-file make up one of the most venerable images in my memory. Physical beauty was indeed common to most of the family. Cousin Mary was the very type of the beauti-ful old lady, with her silver hair and her sweet Southern Irish voice; foreigners must be warned that this resembles what they call a 'brogue' about as little as the speech of a Highland gentleman resembles the jargon of the Glasgow slums. But it was the three daughters whom we knew best.

All three were 'grown up' but in fact much nearer to us in age than any other grown-ups we knew, and all three were strikingly handsome. H., the eldest and the gravest, was a Juno, a dark queen who at certain moments looked like a Jewess. K. was more like a Valkyrie (though all, I think, were good horsewomen) with her father's profile. There was in her face something of the delicate fierceness of a thoroughbred horse, an indignant fineness of nostril, the possibility of an excellent disdain. She had what the vanity of my own sex calls a 'masculine' honesty; no man ever was a truer friend. As for the youngest, G., I can only say that she was the most beautiful woman I have ever seen, per-fect in shape and colour and voice and every movement—but who can describe beauty? The reader may smile at this as the far-off echo of a precocious calf-love, but he will be wrong. There are beauties so unambiguous that they need no lens of that kind to reveal them; they are visible even to the careless and objective eyes of a child. (The first woman who ever spoke to my blood was a dancing mistress at a school that will come in a later chapter.)

In some ways Mountbracken was like our father's house. There too we found the attics, the indoor silences, the endless bookshelves. In the early days, when we were still only a quarter tamed, we often neglected our hostesses and rummaged on our own; it was there that I found Lubbock's *Ants, Bees and Wasps*. But it was also very different. Life there was more spacious and considered than with us, glided like a barge where ours bumped like a cart.

Friends of our own age—boy and girl friends—we had none. In part this is a natural result of boarding-school; children grow up strangers to their next-door neighbours. But much more it was the result of our own obstinate choice. One boy who lived near us attempted every now and then to get to know us. We avoided him by every means in our power. Our lives were already full, and the holidays too short for all the reading, writing, playing, cycling, and talking that we wanted to get through. We resented the appearance of any third party as an infuriating interruption. We resented even more bitterly all attempts (excepting the great and successful attempt made by Mountbracken) to show us hospitality. At the period that I am now speaking of this had not yet become a serious nuisance, but as it became gradually and steadily more serious throughout our schooldays I may be allowed to say a word about it here and to get the subject out of our way. It was the custom of the neighbourhood to give parties which were really dances for adults but to which, none the less, mere schoolboys and schoolgirls were asked. One sees the advantages of this arrangement from

the hostess's point of view; and when the junior guests
know each other well and are free from self-consciousness
perhaps they enjoy themselves. To me these dances were
a torment—of which ordinary shyness made only a part.
It was the false position (which I was well able to realise)
that tormented me; to know that one was regarded as
a child and yet be forced to take part in an essentially
grown-up function, to feel that all the adults present were
being half-mockingly kind and pretending to treat you as
what you were not. Add to this the discomfort of one's
Eton suit and stiff shirt, the aching feet and burning head,
and the mere weariness of being kept up so many hours
after one's usual bedtime. Even adults, I fancy, would not
find an evening party very endurable without the attraction of sex and the attraction of alcohol; and how a small
boy who can neither flirt nor drink should be expected
to enjoy prancing about on a polished floor till the small
hours of the morning, is beyond my conception. I had of
course no notion of the social nexus. I never realised that
certain people were in civility obliged to ask me because
they knew my father or had known my mother. To me it
was all inexplicable, unprovoked persecution; and when,
as often happened, such engagements fell in the last week
of the holidays and wrested from us a huge cantle of hours
in which every minute was worth gold, I positively felt

that I could have torn my hostess limb from limb. Why should she thus pester me? I had never done her any harm, never asked *her* to a party.

My discomforts were aggravated by the totally unnatural behaviour which I thought it my duty to adopt at a dance; and that had come about in a sufficiently amusing way. Reading much and mixing little with children of my own age, I had, before I went to school, developed a vocabulary which must (I now see) have sounded very funny from the lips of a chubby urchin in an Eton jacket. When I brought out my 'long words' adults not unnaturally thought I was showing off. In this they were quite mistaken. I used the only words I knew. The position was indeed the exact reverse of what they supposed; my pride would have been gratified by using such schoolboy slang as I possessed, not at all by using the bookish language which (inevitably in my circumstances) came naturally to my tongue. And there were not lacking adults who would egg me on with feigned interest and feigned seriousness—on and on till the moment at which I suddenly knew I was being laughed at. Then, of course, my mortification was intense; and after one or two such experiences I made it a rigid rule that at 'social functions' (as I secretly called them) I must never on any account speak of any subject in which I felt the slightest interest nor in any words that naturally occurred to me. And I kept my rule only too well; a giggling and gurgling imitation of the vapidest grown-up chatter, a deliberate concealment of all that I really thought and felt under a sort of feeble jocularity and enthusiasm, was henceforth my party manner, assumed as consciously as an actor assumes his role, sustained with unspeakable weariness, and dropped with a groan of relief the moment my brother and I at last tumbled into our cab and the drive home (the only pleasure of the evening) began. It took me years to make the discovery that any real human intercourse could take place at a mixed assembly of people in their good clothes.

I am here struck by the curious mixture of justice and injustice in our lives. We are blamed for our real faults but usually not on the right occasions. I was, no doubt, and was blamed for being a conceited boy; but the blame was usually attached to something in which no conceit was present. Adults often accuse a child of vanity without pausing to discover on what points children in general, or that child in particular, are likely to be vain. Thus it was for years a complete mystery to me that my father should stigmatise as 'affectation' my complaints about the itching and tickling of new underclothes. I see it all now; he had in mind a social legend associating delicacy of skin with refinement and supposed that I was claiming to be unusually refined. In reality I was in simple ignorance of that social legend, and if vanity had come into the matter would have been much prouder of having skin like a sailor. I was being accused of an offence which I lacked resources to commit. I was on another occasion called 'affected' for asking what 'stirabout' was. It is, in fact, a 'low' Irish word for porridge. To certain adults it seems obvious that he who claims not to know the Low must be pretending to be High. Yet the real reason why I asked was that I had never happened to hear the word; had I done so I should have piqued myself on using it.

Oldie's school, you will remember, sank unlamented in summer 1910; new arrangements had to be made for my education. My father now hit upon a plan which filled me with delight. About a mile from the New House rose the large red-brick walls and towers of Campbell College, which had been founded for the express purpose of giving Ulster boys all the advantages of a public school education without the trouble of crossing the Irish Sea. My clever cousin, Uncle Joe's boy, was already there and doing well. It was decided that I should go as a boarder, but I could get an *exeat* to come home every Sunday. I was enchanted. I did not believe that anything Irish, even a school, could be bad; certainly not so bad as all I yet knew of England. To 'Campbell' I accordingly went.

I was at this school for so short a time that I shall attempt no criticism of it. It was very unlike any English public school that I have ever heard of. It had indeed prefects, but the prefects were of no importance. It was nominally divided into 'houses' on the English pattern, but they were mere legal fictions; except for purposes of games (which were not compulsory) no one took any notice of them. The population was socially much more 'mixed' than at most English schools; I rubbed shoulders there with farmers' sons. The boy I most nearly made a friend of was the son of a tradesman who had recently been going the rounds with his father's van because the driver was illiterate and could not keep 'the books'. I much envied him this pleasant occupation, and he, poor fellow, looked back on it as a golden age. 'This time last month, Lewis,' he used to say, 'I wouldn't have been going in to Preparation. I'd have been coming home from my rounds and a wee tea-cloth laid for me at one end of the table and sausages to my tea.'

I am always glad, as a historian, to have known Campbell, for I think it was very much what the great English schools had been before Arnold. There were real fights at Campbell, with seconds, and (I think) betting, and a hundred or more roaring spectators. There was bullying, too, though no serious share of it came my way, and there was no trace of the rigid hierarchy which governs a modern English school; every boy held just the place which his fists and mother-wit could win for him. From my point of view the great drawback was that one had, so to speak, no home. Only a few very senior boys had studies. The rest of us, except when seated at table for meals or in a huge 'preparation room' for evening 'Prep', belonged nowhere. In out-of-school hours one spent one's time either evading or conforming to all those inexplicable movements which a crowd exhibits as it thins here and thickens there, now slackens its pace and now sets like a tide in one particular direction, now seems about to disperse and then clots again. The bare brick passages echoed to a continual tramp of feet, punctuated with catcalls, scrimmages, gusty laughter. One was always 'moving on' or 'hanging about'—in lavatories, in store rooms, in the great hall. It was very like living permanently in a large railway station.

The bullying had this negative merit that it was honest bullying; not bullying conscience-salved and authorised in the *maison tolérée* of the prefectorial system. It was done mainly by gangs; parties of eight or ten boys each who scoured those interminable corridors for prey. Their sorties, though like a whirlwind, were not perceived by the victim till too late; the general, endless confusion and clamour, I suppose, masked them. Sometimes capture

involved serious consequences; two boys whom I knew
were carried off and flogged in some backwater—flogged
in the most disinterested fashion, for their captors had no
personal acquaintance with them; art for art's sake. But
on the only occasion when I was caught myself my fate
was much milder and perhaps odd enough to be worth
recording. When I had come to myself after being dragged
at headlong speed through a labyrinth of passages which
took me beyond all usual landmarks, I found that I was
one of several prisoners in a low, bare room, half-lit (I
think) by a single gas-jet. After a pause to recover their
breath two of the brigands led out the first captive. I now
noticed that a horizontal row of pipes ran along the opposite wall, about three feet from the floor. I was alarmed
but not surprised when the prisoner was forced into a
bending position with his head under the lowest pipe, in
the very posture for execution. But I was very much surprised a moment later. You will remember that the room
was half dark. The two gangsters gave their victim a shove;
and instantly no victim was there. He vanished; without
trace, without sound. It appeared to be sheer black magic.
Another victim was led out; again the posture for a flogging was assumed; again, instead of flogging—dissolution,
atomisation, annihilation. At last my own turn came. I too
received the shove from behind, and found myself falling

through a hole or hatch in the wall into what turned out to be a coal-cellar. Another small boy came hurtling in after me, the door was slammed and bolted behind us, and our captors with a joyous whoop rushed away for more booty. They were, no doubt, playing against a rival gang with whom they would presently compare 'hags'. We were let out again presently, very dirty and rather cramped, but otherwise none the worse.

Much the most important thing that happened to me at Campbell was that I there read *Sohrab and Rustum* in form under an excellent master whom we called Octie. I loved the poem at first sight and have loved it ever since. As the wet fog, in the first line, rose out of the Oxus stream, so out of the whole poem there rose and wrapped me round an exquisite, silvery coolness, a delightful quality of distance and calm, a grave melancholy. I hardly appreciated then, as I have since learned to do, the central tragedy; what enchanted me was the artist in Pekin with his ivory forehead and pale hands, the cypress in the queen's garden, the backward glance at Rustum's youth, the pedlars from Khabul, the hushed Chorasmian waste. Arnold gave me at once (and the best of Arnold gives me still) a sense, not indeed of passionless vision, but of a passionate, silent gazing at things a long way off. And here observe how literature actually works. Parrot critics say that *Sohrab* is a poem for classicists, to be enjoyed only by those who recognise the Homeric echoes. But I, in Octie's form-room (and on Octie be peace) knew nothing of Homer. For me the relation between Arnold and Homer worked the other way; when I came, years later, to read the *Iliad* I liked it partly because it was for me reminiscent of *Sohrab*. Plainly, it does not matter at what point you first break into the system of European poetry. Only keep your ears open and your mouth shut and everything will lead you to everything else in the end—*ogni parte ad ogni parte splende.*

About half-way through my first and only term at Campbell I fell ill and was taken home. My father, for reasons I do not quite know, had become dissatisfied with the school. He had also been attracted by accounts of a preparatory school in the town of Wyvern, though quite unconnected with Wyvern College; especially by the convenience that if I went there my brother and I could still do the journey together. Accordingly I had a blessed six weeks at home, with the Christmas holidays to look forward to at the end and, after that, a new adventure. In a surviving letter my father writes to my brother that I think myself lucky but he 'fears I shall be very lonely before the end of the week'. It is strange that having known me all my life he should have known me so little. During these weeks I slept in his room and was thus freed from solitude during most of those dark hours in which alone solitude was dreadful to me. My brother being absent, he and I could not lead one another into mischief; there was therefore no friction between my father and myself. I remember no other time in my life of such untroubled affection; we were famously snug together. And in the days when he was out, I entered with complete satisfaction into a deeper solitude than I had ever known. The empty house, the empty, silent rooms, were like a refreshing bath after the crowded noise of Campbell. I could read, write, and draw to my heart's content. Curiously enough it is at this time, not in earlier childhood, that I chiefly remember delighting in fairy tales. I fell deeply under the spell of dwarfs—the old bright-hooded, snowy-bearded dwarfs we had in those days before Arthur Rackham sublimed, or Walt Disney vulgarised, the earthmen. I visualised them so intensely that I came to the very frontiers of hallucination; once, walking in the garden, I was for a second not quite sure that a little man had not run past me into the shrubbery. I was faintly alarmed, but it was not like my night-fears. A fear that guarded the road to Faerie was one I could face. No one is a coward at all points.

IV

I BROADEN MY MIND

I struck the board, and cry'd, 'No more; I will abroad'.
What? shall I ever sigh and pine?
My lines and life are free: free as the rode,
Loose as the winde, as large as store.

HERBERT

In January, 1911, just turned thirteen, I set out with my brother to Wyvern, he for the College and I for a preparatory school which we will call Chartres. Thus began what may be called the classic period of our schooldays, the thing we both think of first when boyhood is mentioned. The joint journeys back to school with a reluctant parting at Wyvern station, the hilarious reunion at the same station for the joint journey home, were now the great structural pillars of each year. Growing maturity is marked by the increasing liberties we take with our travelling. At first, on being landed early in the morning at Liverpool, we took the next train south; soon we learned that it was pleasanter

to spend the whole morning in the lounge of the Lime
Street Hotel with our magazines and cigarettes and to proceed to Wyvern by an afternoon train which brought us
there at the latest permitted moment. Soon too we gave up
the magazines; we made the discovery (some people never
make it) that real books can be taken on a journey and that
hours of golden reading can so be added to its other
delights. (It is important to acquire early in life the power
of reading sense wherever you happen to be. I first read
Tamburlaine while travelling from Lame to Belfast in a
thunderstorm, and first read Browning's *Paracelsus* by a
candle which went out and had to be relit whenever a big
battery fired in a pit below me, which I think it did every
four minutes all that night.) The homeward journey was
even more festal. It had an invariable routine: first the supper at a restaurant—it was merely poached eggs and tea but
to us the tables of the gods—then the visit to the old Empire
(there were still music halls in those days)—and after that
the journey to the Landing Stage, the sight of great and
famous ships, the departure, and once more the blessed salt
on our lips.

The smoking was of course, as my father would have
said, 'surreptitious'; not so the visit to the Empire. He was
no Puritan about such matters, and often of a Saturday
night would take us to the Belfast Hippodrome. I recog-

nise now that I never had the taste for vaudeville which
he shared with my brother. At the time I supposed myself
to be enjoying the show, but I was mistaken. All those
antics lie dead in my memory and are incapable of rousing
the least vibration even of reminiscent pleasure; whereas
the pain of sympathy and vicarious humiliation which I
felt when a 'turn' failed is still vivid. What I enjoyed was
merely the et cetera of the show, the bustle and lights, the
sense of having a night out, the good spirits of my father
in his holiday mood, and—above all—the admirable cold
supper to which we came back at about ten o'clock. For
this was also the classical age of our domestic cookery, the
age of one Annie Strahan. There were certain 'raised pies'
set on that table of which a modern English boy has no
conception, and which even then would have astonished
those who knew only the poor counterfeits sold in shops.

Chartres, a tall, white building further up the hill than
the College, was a smallish school with less than twenty
boarders; but it was quite unlike Oldie's. Here indeed my
education really began. The Headmaster, whom we called
Tubbs, was a clever and patient teacher; under him I rapidly found my feet in Latin and English and even began to
be looked on as a promising candidate for a scholarship
at the College. The food was good (though of course we
grumbled at it) and we were well cared for. On the whole

I got on well with my schoolfellows, though we had our full share of those lifelong friendships and irreconcilable factions and deadly quarrels and final settlements and glorious revolutions which made up so much of the life of a small boy, and in which I came out sometimes at the bottom and sometimes at the top.

Wyvern itself healed my quarrel with England. The great blue plain below us and, behind, those green, peaked hills, so mountainous in form and yet so manageably small in size, became almost at once my delight. And Wyvern Priory was the first building that I ever perceived to be beautiful. And at Chartres I made my first real friends. But there, too, something far more important happened to me: I ceased to be a Christian.

The chronology of this disaster is a little vague, but I know for certain that it had not begun when I went there and that the process was complete very shortly after I left. I will try to set down what I know of the conscious causes and what I suspect of the unconscious.

Most reluctantly, venturing no blame, and as tenderly as I would at need reveal some error in my own mother, I must begin with dear Miss C., the Matron. No school ever had a better Matron, more skilled and comforting to boys in sickness, or more cheery and companionable to boys in health. She was one of the most selfless people I have ever known. We all loved her; I, the orphan, especially. Now it so happened that Miss C., who seemed old to me, was still in her spiritual immaturity, still hunting, with the eagerness of a soul that had a touch of angelic quality in it, for a truth and a way of life. Guides were even rarer then than now. She was (as I should now put it) floundering in the mazes of Theosophy, Rosicrucianism, Spiritualism; the whole Anglo-American Occultist tradition. Nothing was further from her intention than to destroy my faith; she could not tell that the room into which she brought this candle was full of gunpowder. I had never heard of such things before; never, except in a nightmare or a fairy tale, conceived of spirits other than God and men. I had loved to read of strange sights and other worlds and unknown modes of being, but never with the slightest belief; even the phantom dwarf had only flashed on my mind for a moment. It is a great mistake to suppose that children believe the things they imagine; and I, long familiar with the whole imaginary world of Animal-Land and India (which I could not possibly believe in since I knew I was one of its creators) was as little likely as any child to make that mistake. But now, for the first time, there burst upon me the idea that there might be real marvels all about us, that the visible world might be only a curtain to conceal huge realms uncharted by my very simple theology. And that started in me something with which, on and off, I have had plenty of trouble since—the desire for the preternatural, simply as such, the passion for the Occult. Not everyone has this disease; those who have will know what I mean. I once tried to describe it in a novel. It is a spiritual lust; and like the lust of the body it has the fatal power of making everything else in the world seem uninteresting while it lasts. It is probably this passion, more even than the desire for power, which makes magicians. But the result of Miss C.'s conversation did not stop there. Little by little, unconsciously, unintentionally, she loosened the whole framework, blunted all the sharp edges, of my belief. The vagueness, the merely speculative character, of all this Occultism began to spread—yes, and to spread *deliciously*—to the stem truths of the creed. The whole thing became a matter of speculation: I was soon (in the famous words) 'altering 'I believe' to 'one does feel''. And oh, the relief of it! Those moonlit nights in the dormitory at Belsen faded far away. From the tyrannous noon of revelation I passed into the cool evening twilight of Higher Thought, where there was nothing to be obeyed, and nothing to be believed except what was either comforting or exciting. I do not mean that Miss C. did this; better say that the Enemy did this in me, taking occasion from things she innocently said.

One reason why the Enemy found this so easy was that, without knowing it, I was already desperately anxious to get rid of my religion; and that for a reason worth recording. By a sheer mistake—and I still believe it to have been an honest mistake—in spiritual technique I had rendered my private practice of that religion a quite intolerable burden. It came about in this way. Like everyone else I had been told as a child that one must not only say one's prayers but think about what one was saying. Accordingly, when (at Oldie's) I came to a serious belief, I tried to put this into practice. At first it seemed plain sailing. But soon the false conscience (St Paul's 'Law', Herbert's 'prattler') came into play. One had no sooner reached 'Amen' than it whispered, 'Yes. But are you sure you were really thinking about what you said?'; then, more subtly, 'Were you, for example, thinking about it as well as you *did* last night?' The answer, for reasons I did not then understand, was nearly always No. 'Very well,' said the voice, 'hadn't you, then, better try it over again?' And one obeyed; but of course with no assurance that the second attempt would be any better.

To these nagging suggestions my reaction was, on the whole, the most foolish I could have adopted. I set myself a standard. No clause of my prayer was to be allowed to pass muster unless it was accompanied by what I called a 'realisation', by which I meant a certain vividness of the imagination and the affections. My nightly task was to produce by sheer willpower a phenomenon which willpower could never produce, which was so ill-defined that I could never say with absolute confidence whether it had occurred, and which, even when it did occur, was of very mediocre spiritual value. If only someone had read to me old Walter Hilton's warning that we must never in prayer strive to extort 'by maistry' what God does not give! But no one did; and night after night, dizzy with desire for sleep and often in a kind of despair, I endeavoured to pump up my 'realisations'. The thing threatened to become an infinite regress. One began of course by praying for good 'realisations'. But had that preliminary prayer itself been 'realised'? This question I think I still had enough sense to dismiss; otherwise it might have been as difficult to begin my prayers as to end them. How it all comes back! The cold oil-cloth, the quarters chiming, the night slipping past, the sickening, hopeless weariness. This was the burden from which I longed with soul and body to escape. It had already brought me to such a pass that the nightly torment projected its gloom over the whole evening, and I dreaded bedtime as if I were a chronic sufferer from insomnia. Had I pursued the same road much further I think I should have gone mad.

This ludicrous burden of false duties in prayer provided, of course, an unconscious motive for wishing to shuffle off the Christian faith; but about the same time, or a little later, conscious causes of doubt arose. One came from reading the classics. Here, especially in Virgil, one was presented with a mass of religious ideas; and all teachers and editors took it for granted from the outset that these religious ideas were sheer illusion. No one ever attempted to show in what sense Christianity fulfilled Paganism or Paganism prefigured Christianity. The accepted position seemed to be that religions were normally a mere farrago of nonsense, though our own, by a fortunate exception, was exactly true. The other religions were not even explained, in the earlier Christian fashion, as the work of devils. That I might, conceivably, have been brought to believe. But the impression I got was that religion in general, though utterly false, was a natural growth, a kind of endemic nonsense into which humanity tended to blunder. In the midst of a thousand such religions stood our own, the thousand and first, labelled True. But on what grounds could I believe in this exception? It obviously was in some general sense the same kind of thing as all the rest. Why was it so differently treated? Need I, at any rate, continue to treat it differently? I was very anxious not to.

In addition to this, and equally working against my

faith, there was in me a deeply ingrained pessimism; a pessimism, by that time, much more of intellect than of temper. I was now by no means unhappy; but I had very definitely formed the opinion that the universe was, in the main, a rather regrettable institution. I am well aware that some will feel disgust and some will laugh, at the idea of a loutish, well-fed boy in an Eton collar, passing an unfavourable judgement on the cosmos. They may be right in either reaction, but no more right because I wore an Eton collar. They are forgetting what boyhood felt like from within. Dates are not so important as people believe. I fancy that most of those who think at all have done a great deal of thinking in the first fourteen years. As to the sources of my pessimism, the reader will remember that though in many ways most fortunate, yet I had very early in life met a great dismay. But I am now inclined to think that the seeds of pessimism were sown before my mother's death. Ridiculous as it may sound, I believe that the clumsiness of my hands was at the root of the matter. How could this be? Not, certainly, that a child says, 'I can't cut a straight line with a pair of scissors, therefore the universe is evil.' Childhood has no such power of generalisation and is not (to do it justice) so silly. Nor did my clumsiness produce what is ordinarily called an Inferiority Complex. I was not comparing myself with other boys;

my defeats occurred in solitude. What they really bred in me was a deep (and, of course, inarticulate) sense of resistance or opposition on the part of inanimate things. Even that makes it too abstract and adult. Perhaps I had better call it a settled expectation that everything would do what you did not want it to do. Whatever you wanted to remain straight, would bend; whatever you tried to bend would fly back to the straight; all knots which you wished to be firm would come untied; all knots you wanted to untie would remain firm. It is not possible to put it into language without making it comic, and I have indeed no wish to see it (now) except as something comic. But it is perhaps just these early experiences which are so fugitive and, to an adult, so grotesque, that give the mind its earliest bias, its habitual sense of what is or is not plausible.

There was another predisposing factor. Though the son of a prosperous man—a man by our present tax-ridden standards almost incredibly comfortable and secure—I had heard ever since I could remember, and believed, that adult life was to be an unremitting struggle in which the best I could hope for was to avoid the workhouse by extreme exertion. My father's highly coloured statements on such matters had sunk deeply into my mind; and I never thought to check them by the very obvious fact that most of the adults I actually knew seemed to be living very comfortable lives. I remember summing up what I took to be our destiny, in conversation with my best friend at Chartres, by the formula, 'Term, holidays, term, holidays, till we leave school, and then work, work, work till we die.' Even if I had been free from this delusion, I think I should still have seen grounds for pessimism. One's views, even at that age, are not wholly determined by one's own momentary situation; even a boy can recognise that there is desert all round him though he, for the nonce, sits in an oasis. I was, in my ineffective way, a tender-hearted creature; perhaps the most murderous feelings I ever entertained were towards an under master at Chartres who forbade me to give to a beggar at the school gate. Add to this that my early reading — not only Wells but Sir Robert Ball — had lodged very firmly in my imagination the vastness and cold of space, the littleness of Man. It is not strange that I should feel the universe to be a menacing and unfriendly place. Several years before I read Lucretius I felt the force of his argument (and it is surely the strongest of all) for atheism —

Nequaquam nobis divinitus esse paratam
Naturam rerum; tanta stat praedita culpa

Had God designed the world, it would not be
A world so frail and faulty as we see.

You may ask how I combined this directly Atheistical thought, this great 'Argument from Undesign' with my Occultist fancies. I do not think I achieved any logical connection between them. They swayed me in different moods, and had only this in common, that both made against Christianity. And so, little by little, with fluctuations which I cannot now trace, I became an apostate, dropping my faith with no sense of loss but with the greatest relief.

My stay at Chartres lasted from the spring term of 1911 till the end of the summer term 1913, and, as I have said, I cannot give an accurate chronology, between those dates, of my slow apostasy. In other respects the period is divided into two; about half-way through it a much loved under master, and the even more loved Matron, left at the same time. From that day onwards there was a sharp decline; not, indeed, in apparent happiness but in solid good. Dear Miss C. had been the occasion of much good to me as well as of evil. For one thing, by awakening my affections, she had done something to defeat that antisentimental inhibition which my early experience had bred in me. Nor would I deny that in all her 'Higher Thought', disastrous though its main effect on me was, there were elements of real and disinterested spirituality by which I benefited. Unfortunately, once her presence was withdrawn, the good effects withered and the bad ones remained. The change of masters was even more obviously for the worse. 'Sirrah', as we called him, had been an admirable influence. He was what I would now describe as a wise madcap: a boisterous, boyish, hearty man, well able to keep his authority while yet mixing with us almost as one of ourselves, an untidy, rollicking man without a particle of affectation. He communicated (what I very much needed) a sense of the gusto with which life ought, wherever possible, to be taken. I fancy it was on a run with him in the sleet that I first discovered how bad weather is to be treated—as a rough joke, a romp. He was succeeded by a young gentleman just down from the University whom we may call Pogo. Pogo was a very minor edition of a Saki, perhaps even a Wodehouse, hero. Pogo was a wit, Pogo was a dressy man, Pogo was a man about town, Pogo was even a lad. After a week or so of hesitation (for his temper was uncertain) we fell at his feet and adored. Here was sophistication, glossy all over, and (dared one believe it?) ready to impart sophistication to us.

We became—at least I became—dressy. It was the age of the 'knut': of 'spread' ties with pins in them, of very low cut coats and trousers worn very high to show startling socks, and brogue shoes with immensely wide laces.

Something of all this had already trickled to me from the College through my brother, who was now becoming sufficiently senior to aspire to knuttery. Pogo completed the process. A more pitiful ambition for a lout of an overgrown fourteen-year-old with a shilling a week pocket money could hardly be imagined; the more so since I am one of those on whom Nature has laid the doom that whatever they buy and whatever they wear they will always look as if they had come out of an old clothes shop. I cannot even now remember without embarrassment the concern that I then felt about pressing my trousers and (filthy habit) plastering my hair with oil. A new element had entered my life: Vulgarity. Up till now I had committed nearly every other sin and folly within my power, but I had not yet been flashy.

These hobble-de-hoy fineries were, however, only a small part of our new sophistication. Pogo was a great theatrical authority. We soon knew all the latest songs. We soon knew all about the famous actresses of that age— Lily Elsie, Gertie Millar, Zena Dare. Pogo was a fund of information about their private lives. We learned from him all the latest jokes; where we did not understand he was ready to give us help. He explained many things. After a term of Pogo's society one had the feeling of being not twelve weeks but twelve years older.

How gratifying, and how edifying, it would be if I could trace to Pogo all my slips from virtue and wind up by pointing the moral; how much harm a loose-talking young man can do to innocent boys! Unfortunately this would be false. It is quite true that at this time I underwent a violent, and wholly successful, assault of sexual temptation. But this is amply accounted for by the age I had then reached and by my recent, in a sense my deliberate, withdrawal of myself from Divine protection. I do not believe Pogo had anything to do with it. The mere facts of generation I had learned long ago, from another boy, when I was too young to feel much more than a scientific interest in them. What attacked me through Pogo was not the Flesh (I had that of my own) but the World: the desire for glitter, swagger, distinction, the desire to be in the know. He gave little help, if any, in destroying my chastity, but he made sad work of certain humble and childlike and self-forgetful qualities which (I think) had remained with me till that moment. I began to labour very hard to make myself into a fop, a cad, and a snob.

Pogo's communications, however much they helped to vulgarise my mind, had no such electric effect on my senses as the dancing mistress, nor as Bekker's *Charicles*, which was given me for a prize. I never thought that dancing mistress as beautiful as my cousin G., but she was the first woman I ever 'looked upon to lust after her'; assuredly through no fault of her own. A gesture, a tone of the voice, may in these matters have unpredictable results. When the schoolroom on the last night of the winter term was decorated for a dance, she paused, lifted a flag, and, remarking, 'I love the smell of bunting,' pressed it to her face—and I was undone.

You must not suppose that this was a romantic passion. The passion of my life, as the next chapter will show, belonged to a wholly different region. What I felt for the dancing mistress was sheer appetite; the prose and not the poetry of the Flesh. I did not feel at all like a knight devoting himself to a lady; I was much more like a Turk looking at a Circassian whom he could not afford to buy. I knew quite well what I wanted. It is common, by the way, to assume that such an experience produces a feeling of guilt, but it did not do so in me. And I may as well say here that the feeling of guilt, save where a moral offence happened also to break the code of honour or had consequences which excited my pity, was a thing which at that time I hardly knew. It took me as long to acquire inhibitions as others (they say) have taken to get rid of them. That is why I often find myself at such cross-purposes with the modern world: I have been a converted Pagan living among apostate Puritans.

I would be sorry if the reader passed too harsh a judgement on Pogo. As I now see it, he was not too old to have charge of boys but too young. He was only an adolescent himself, still immature enough to be delightedly 'grown up' and naïve enough to enjoy our greater naïveté. And there was a real friendliness in him. He was moved partly by that to tell us all he knew or thought he knew. And now, as Herodotus would say, 'Good-bye to Pogo.'

Meanwhile, side by side with my loss of faith, of virtue, and of simplicity, something quite different was going on. It will demand a new chapter.

V

RENAISSANCE

> So is there in us a world of love to somewhat,
> though we know not what in the world that
> should be.
>
> TRAHERNE

I do not much believe in the Renaissance as generally
described by historians. The more I look into the evidence
the less trace I find of that vernal rapture which is supposed
to have swept Europe in the fifteenth century. I half suspect
that the glow in the historians' pages has a different source,
that each is remembering, and projecting, his own personal
Renaissance; that wonderful reawakening which comes to
most of us when puberty is complete. It is properly called
a re-birth not a birth, a reawakening not a wakening,
because in many of us, besides being a new thing, it is also
the recovery of things we had in childhood and lost when
we became boys. For boyhood is very like the 'dark ages'
not as they were but as they are represented in bad, short

histories. The dreams of childhood and those of adolescence may have much in common; between them, often, boyhood stretches like an alien territory in which everything (ourselves included) has been greedy, cruel, noisy, and prosaic, in which the imagination has slept and the most unideal senses and ambitions have been restlessly, even maniacally, awake.

In my own life it was certainly so. My childhood is at unity with the rest of my life; my boyhood not so. Many of the books that pleased me as a child, please me still; nothing but necessity would make me re-read most of the books that I read at Oldie's or at Campbell. From that point of view it is all a sandy desert. The authentic 'Joy' (as I tried to describe it in an earlier chapter) had vanished from my life: so completely that not even the memory or the desire of it remained. The reading of *Sohrab* had not given it to me. Joy is distinct not only from pleasure in general but even from aesthetic pleasure. It must have the stab, the pang, the inconsolable longing.

This long winter broke up in a single moment, fairly early in my time at Chartres. Spring is the inevitable image, but this was not gradual like Nature's springs. It was as if the Arctic itself, all the deep layers of secular ice, should change not in a week nor in an hour, but instantly, into a landscape of grass and primroses and orchards in bloom, deafened with bird songs and astir with running water. I can lay my hand on the very moment; there is hardly any fact I know so well, though I cannot date it. Someone must have left in the schoolroom a literary periodical: *The Bookman*, perhaps, or the *Times Literary Supplement*. My eye fell upon a headline and a picture, carelessly, expecting nothing. A moment later, as the poet says, 'The sky had turned round.'

What I had read was the words *Siegfried and the Twilight of the Gods*. What I had seen was one of Arthur Rackham's illustrations to that volume. I had never heard of Wagner, nor of Siegfried. I thought the Twilight of the Gods means the twilight in which the gods lived. How did I know, at once and beyond question, that this was no Celtic, or silvan, or terrestrial twilight? But so it was. Pure 'Northernness' engulfed me: a vision of huge, clear spaces hanging above the Atlantic in the endless twilight of Northern summer, remoteness, severity . . . and almost at the same moment I knew that I had met this before, long, long ago (it hardly seems longer now) in *Tegner's Drapa*, that Siegfried (whatever it might be) belonged to the same world as Balder and the sunward-sailing cranes. And with that plunge back into my own past there arose at once, almost like heartbreak, the memory of Joy itself, the knowledge that I had once had what I had now lacked for years, that I was returning at last from exile and desert lands to my own country; and the distance of the Twilight of the Gods and the distance of my own past Joy, both unattainable, flowed together into a single, unendurable sense of desire and loss, which suddenly became one with the loss of the whole experience, which, as I now stared round that dusty schoolroom like a man recovering from unconsciousness, had already vanished, had eluded me at the very moment when I could first say *It is.* And at once I knew (with fatal knowledge) that to 'have it again' was the supreme and only important object of desire.

After this everything played into my hands. One of my father's many presents to us boys had been a gramophone. Thus at the moment when my eyes fell on the words *Siegfried and the Twilight of the Gods,* gramophone catalogues were already one of my favourite forms of reading; but I had never remotely dreamed that the records from Grand Opera with their queer German or Italian names could have anything to do with me. Nor did I for a week or two think so now. But then I was assailed from a new quarter. A magazine called *The Soundbox* was doing synopses of great operas week by week, and it now did the whole *Ring.* I read in a rapture and discovered who Siegfried was and what was the 'twilight' of the gods. I could contain myself no longer—I began a poem, a heroic poem on the Wagnerian version of the Niblung story. My only source was the abstracts in *The Soundbox,* and I was so ignorant that I made Alberich rhyme with *ditch* and Mime with *time.* My model was Pope's *Odyssey* and the poem began (with some mixture of mythologies)

> *Descend to earth, descend, celestial Nine*
> *And chant the ancient legends of the Rhine . . .*

Since the fourth book had carried me only as far as the last scene of *The Rheingold,* the reader will not be surprised to hear that the poem was never finished. But it was not a waste of time, and I can still see just what it did for me and where it began to do it. The first three books (I may, perhaps, at this distance of time, say it without vanity) are really not at all bad for a boy. At the beginning of the unfinished fourth it goes all to pieces; and that is exactly the point at which I really began to try to make poetry. Up to then, if my lines rhymed and scanned and got on with the story I asked no more. Now, at the beginning of the fourth, I began to try to convey some of the intense excitement I was feeling, to look for expressions which would not merely state but suggest. Of course I failed, lost my prosaic clarity, spluttered, gasped, and presently fell silent; but I had learned what writing means.

All this time I had still not heard a note of Wagner's music, though the very shape of the printed letters of his name had become to me a magical symbol. Next holidays, in the dark, crowded shop of T. Edens Osborne (on whom be peace), I first heard a record of the *Ride of the Valkyries.* They laugh at it nowadays, and, indeed, wrenched from its context to make a concert piece, it may be a poor thing. But I had this in common with Wagner, that I was thinking not of concert pieces but of heroic drama. To a boy already crazed with 'the Northernness', whose highest musical experience had been Sullivan, the *Ride* came like a thunderbolt. From that moment Wagnerian records (principally from the *Ring,* but also from *Lohengrin* and *Parsifal)* became the chief drain on my pocket money and the presents I invariably asked for. My general appreciation of music was not, at first, much altered. 'Music' was one thing, 'Wagnerian music' quite another, and there was no common measure between them; it was not a new pleasure but a new kind of pleasure, if indeed *pleasure* is the right word, rather than trouble, ecstasy, astonishment, 'a conflict of sensations without name'.

That summer our cousin H. (you remember, I hope, Cousin Quartus' eldest daughter, the dark Juno, the queen of Olympus), who was now married, asked us to spend some weeks with her on the outskirts of Dublin, in

Dundrum. There, on her drawing-room table, I found the very book which had started the whole affair and which I had never dared to hope I should see, *Siegfried and the Twilight of the Gods* illustrated by Arthur Rackham. His pictures, which seemed to me then to be the very music made visible, plunged me a few fathoms deeper into my delight. I have seldom coveted anything as I coveted that book; and when I heard that there was a cheaper edition at fifteen shillings (though the sum was to me almost mythological) I knew I could never rest till it was mine. I got it in the end, largely because my brother went shares with me, purely through kindness, as I now see and then more than half suspected, for he was not enslaved by the Northernness. With a generosity which I was even then half ashamed to accept, he sank in what must have seemed to him a mere picture-book seven and sixpence for which he knew a dozen better uses.

Although this affair will already seem to some readers undeserving of the space I have given it, I cannot continue my story at all without noting some of its bearings on the rest of my life.

First, you will misunderstand everything unless you realise that, at the time, Asgard and the Valkyries seemed to me incomparably more important than anything else in my experience—than the Matron Miss C., or the dancing mistress, or my chances of a scholarship. More shockingly, they seemed much more important than my steadily growing doubts about Christianity. This may have been—in part, no doubt, was—penal blindness; yet that might not be the whole story. If the Northernness seemed then a bigger thing than my religion, that may partly have been because my attitude towards it contained elements which my religion ought to have contained and did not. It was not itself a new religion, for it contained no trace of belief and imposed no duties. Yet unless I am greatly mistaken there was in it something very like adoration, some kind of quite disinterested self-abandonment to an object which securely claimed this by simply being the object it was. We are taught in the Prayer Book to 'give thanks to God for His great glory', as if we owed Him more thanks for being what He necessarily is than for any particular benefit He confers upon us; and so indeed we do and to know God is to know this. But I had been far from any such experience; I came far nearer to feeling this about the Norse gods whom I disbelieved in than I had ever done about the true God while I believed. Sometimes I can almost think that I was sent back to the false gods there to acquire some capacity for worship against the day when the true God should recall me to Himself. Not that I might not have learned this sooner and more safely, in ways I shall now never know, without apostasy, but that Divine punishments are also mercies, and particular good is worked out of particular evil, and the penal blindness made sanative.

Secondly, this imaginative Renaissance almost at once produced a new appreciation of external nature. At first, I think, this was parasitic on the literary and musical experiences. On that holiday at Dundrum, cycling among the Wicklow mountains, I was always involuntarily looking for scenes that might belong to the Wagnerian world, here a steep hillside covered with firs where Mime might meet Sieglinde, there a sunny glade where Siegfried might listen to the bird, or presently a dry valley of rocks where the lithe scaly body of Fafner might emerge from its cave. But soon (I cannot say how soon) nature ceased to be a mere reminder of the books, became herself the medium of the real joy. I do not say she ceased to be a reminder. All Joy reminds. It is never a possession, always a desire for something longer ago or further away or still 'about to be'. But Nature and the books now became equal reminders, joint reminders, of—well, of whatever it is. I came no nearer to what some would regard as the only genuine love of nature, the studious love which will make a man a botanist or an ornithologist. It was the mood of a scene that mattered to me; and in tasting that mood my skin and nose were as busy as my eyes.

Thirdly, I passed on from Wagner to everything else
I could get hold of about Norse mythology, *Myths of
the Norsemen, Myths and Legends of the Teutonic Race,*
Mallet's *Northern Antiquities.* I became knowledgeable.
From these books again and again I received the stab of
Joy. I did not yet notice that it was, very gradually, becoming rarer. I did not yet reflect on the difference between it
and the merely intellectual satisfaction of getting to know
the Eddaic universe. If I could at this time have found
anyone to teach me Old Norse I believe I would have
worked at it hard.

And finally, the change I had undergone introduces a
new difficulty into the writing of this present book. From
that first moment in the schoolroom at Chartres my
secret, imaginative life began to be so important and so
distinct from my outer life that I almost have to tell two
separate stories. The two lives do not seem to influence
each other at all. Where there are hungry wastes, starving
for Joy, in the one, the other may be full of cheerful bustle
and success; or again, where the outer life is miserable, the
other may be brimming over with ecstasy. By the imaginative life I here mean only my life as concerned with Joy —
including in the outer life much that would ordinarily be
called imagination, as, for example, much of my reading,
and all my erotic or ambitious fantasies; for these are self-

regarding. Even Animal-Land and India belong to the 'Outer'.

But they were no longer Animal-Land and India; some time in the late eighteenth century (their eighteenth century, not ours) they had been united into the single state of Boxen, which yields, oddly, an adjective *Boxonian*, not *Boxenian* as you might expect. By a wise provision they retained their separate kings but had a common legislative assembly, the Damerfesk. The electoral system was democratic, but this mattered very much less than in England, for the Damerfesk was never doomed to one fixed meeting place. The joint sovereigns could summon it anywhere, say at the tiny fishing village of Danphabel (the Clovelly of Northern Animal-Land, nestling at the foot of the mountains) or in the island of Piscia; and since the Court knew the sovereigns' choice earlier than anyone else, all local accommodation would be booked before a private member got wind of the matter, nor, if he reached the session, had he the least assurance that it would not be moved elsewhere as soon as he arrived. Hence we hear of a certain member who had never actually sat in the Damerfesk at all except on one fortunate occasion when it met in his home town. The records sometimes call this assembly the Parliament, but that is misleading. It had only a single chamber, and the kings presided. At the period which I know best the effective control, however, was not in their hands but in those of an all-important functionary known as the Littlemaster (you must pronounce this all as one word with the accent on the first syllable—like *jerrybuilder*). The Littlemaster was a Prime Minister, a judge, and if not always Commander-in-Chief (the records waver on this point) certainly always a member of the General Staff. Such at least were the powers he wielded when I last visited Boxen. They may have been encroachments, for the office was held at that time by a man—or to speak more accurately, a Frog—of powerful personality. Lord Big brought to his task one rather unfair advantage; he had been the tutor of the two young kings and continued to hold over them a quasi-parental authority. Their spasmodic efforts to break his yoke were, unhappily, more directed to the evasion of his enquiry into their private pleasures than to any serious political end. As a result Lord Big, immense in size, resonant of voice, chivalrous (he was the hero of innumerable duels), stormy, eloquent, and impulsive, almost was the State. The reader will divine a certain resemblance between the life of the two kings under Lord Big and our own life under our father. He will be right. But Big was not, in origin, simply our father first batrachised and then caricatured in some directions and glorified in others. He was in many ways a prophetic portrait of Sir Winston Churchill as Sir Winston Churchill came to be during the last war; I have indeed seen photographs of that great statesman in which, to anyone who has known Boxen, the frog element was unmistakable. This was not our only anticipation of the real world. Lord Big's most consistent opponent, the gadfly that always got inside his armour, was a certain small brown bear, a lieutenant in the Navy; and believe me or believe me not, Lieutenant James Bar was almost exactly like Mr John Betjeman, whose acquaintance I could not then have made. Ever since I have done so, I have been playing Lord Big to his James Bar.

The interesting thing about the resemblance between Lord Big and my father is that such reflections of the real world had not been the germ out of which Boxen grew. They were more numerous as it drew nearer to its end, a sign of over-ripeness or even the beginning of decay. Go back a little and you will not find them. The two sovereigns who allowed themselves to be dominated by Lord Big were King Benjamin VIII of Animal-Land and Rajah Hawki (I think, VI) of India. They had much in common with my brother and myself. But their fathers, the elder Benjamin and the elder Hawki, had not. The Fifth Hawki is a shadowy figure; but the Seventh Benjamin (a rabbit, as you will have guessed) is a rounded character. I can see him still—the heaviest-jowled and squarest-builded of all rabbits, very fat in his later years, most shabbily and unroyally clad in his loose brown coat and baggy checked trousers, yet not without a certain dignity which could, on occasion, take disconcerting forms. His earlier life had been dominated by the belief that he could be both a king and an amateur detective. He never succeeded in the latter role, partly because the chief enemy whom he was pursuing (Mr Baddlesmere) was not really a criminal at all but a lunatic—a complication which would have thrown out the plans of Sherlock Holmes himself. But he very often got himself kidnapped, sometimes for longish periods, and caused great anxiety to his Court (we do not learn that his colleague, Hawki V, shared this). Once, on his return from such a misadventure, he had great difficulty in establishing his identity; Baddlesmere had dyed him and the familiar brown figure reappeared as a piebald rabbit. Finally (what will not boys think of?) he was a very early experimenter with what has since been called artificial insemination. The judgement of history cannot pronounce him either a good rabbit or a good king; but he was not a nonentity. He ate prodigiously.

And now that I have opened the gate, all the Boxonians, like the ghosts in Homer, come clamouring for mention.

But they must be denied it. Readers who have built a world would rather tell of their own than hear of mine; those who have not would perhaps be bewildered and repelled. Nor had Boxen any connection with Joy. I have mentioned it at all only because to omit it would have been to misinterpret this period of my life.

One caution must here be repeated. I have been describing a life in which, plainly, imagination of one sort or another played the dominant part. Remember that it never involved the least grain of belief; I never mistook imagination for reality. About the Northernness no such question could arise: it was essentially a desire and implied the absence of its object. And Boxen we never could believe in, for we had made it. No novelist (in that sense) believes in his own characters.

At the end of the Summer Term 1913 I won a classical entrance scholarship to Wyvern College.

VI

BLOODERY

Any way for Heaven sake
So I were out of your whispering.

WEBSTER

Now that we have done with Chartres we may call
Wyvern College simply Wyvern, or more simply still, as
Wyvernians themselves call it, the Coll.

Going to the Coll was the most exciting thing that had
yet happened in my outer life. At Chartres we had lived
under the shadow of the Coll. We were often taken there
to see matches or sports or the finish of the great Goldbury
Run. These visits turned our heads. The crowd of boys
older than oneself, their dazzling air of sophistication,
scraps of their esoteric talk overheard, were like Park Lane
in the old 'Season' to a girl who is to be a *debutante* next
year. Above all, the Bloods, the adored athletes and prefects, were an embodiment of all worldly pomp, power, and
glory. Beside them Pogo shrank into insignificance; what is

a Master compared with a Blood? The whole school was a great temple for the worship of these mortal gods; and no boy ever went there more prepared to worship them than I.

If you have not been at such a school as Wyvern, you may ask what a *Blood* is. He is a member of the school aristocracy. Foreign readers must clearly understand that this aristocracy has nothing whatsoever to do with the social position of the boys in the outer world. Boys of good, or wealthy, family are no more likely to be in it than anyone else; the only nobleman in my House at Wyvern never became a Blood. Shortly before my time there the son of a very queer customer had been at least on the fringe of Bloodery. The qualifying condition for Bloodery is that one should have been at the school for a considerable time. This by itself will not get you in, but newness will certainly exclude you. The most important qualification is athletic prowess. Indeed if this is sufficiently brilliant it makes you a Blood automatically. If it is a little less brilliant, then good looks and personality will help. So, of course, will fashion, as fashion is understood at your school. A wise candidate for Bloodery will wear the right clothes, use the right slang, admire the right things, laugh at the right jokes. And of course, as in the outer world, those on the fringes of the privileged class can, and do, try to worm their way into it by all the usual arts of pleasing.

At some schools, I am told, there is a sort of dyarchy. An aristocracy of Bloods, supported or at least tolerated by popular sentiment, stands over against an official ruling class of prefects appointed by the Masters. I believe they usually appoint it from the highest form, so that it has some claim to be an intelligentsia. It was not so at the Coll. Those who were made prefects were nearly all Bloods and they did not have to be in any particular form. Theoretically (though I do not suppose this would ever happen) the dunce at the bottom of the lowest form could have been made the captain—in our language, the Head—of the Coll. We thus had only a single governing class, in whom every kind of power, privilege, and prestige were united. Those to whom the hero-worship of their juniors would in any case have gone, and those whose astuteness and ambition would under any system have enabled them to rise, were the same whom the official power of the Masters supported. Their position was emphasised by special liberties, clothes, priorities, and dignities which affected every side of school life. This, you will see, makes a pretty strong class. But it was strengthened *still* further by a factor which distinguishes school from ordinary life. In a country governed by an oligarchy, huge numbers of people, and among them some very stirring spirits, know they can never hope to get into that oligarchy; it may therefore be worth their while to attempt a revolution. At the Coll the lowest social class of all were too young, therefore too weak, to dream of revolt. In the middle class—boys who were no longer fags but not yet Bloods—those who alone had physical strength and popularity enough to qualify them as leaders of a revolution were already beginning to hope for Bloodery themselves. It suited them better to accelerate their social progress by courting the existing Bloods than to risk a revolt which, in the unlikely event of its succeeding, would destroy the very prize they were longing to share. And if at last they despaired of ever doing so—why, by that time their schooldays were nearly over. Hence the Wyvernian constitution was unbreakable. Schoolboys have often risen against their Masters; I doubt if there has ever been or ever can be a revolt against Bloods.

It is not, then, surprising if I went to the Coll prepared to worship. Can any adult aristocracy present the World to us in quite such an alluring form as the hierarchy of a public school? Every motive for prostration is brought to bear at once on the mind of the New Boy when he sees a Blood; the natural respect of the thirteen-year-old for the nineteen-year-old, the fan's feeling for a film-star, the suburban woman's feeling for a duchess, the newcomer's awe in the presence of the Old Hand, the street urchin's dread of the police.

One's first hours at a public school are unforgettable. Our House was a tall, narrow stone building (and, by the way, the only house in the place which was not an architectural nightmare) rather like a ship. The deck on which we chiefly lived consisted of two very dark stone corridors at right angles to one another. The doors off them opened into the studies—little rooms about six feet square, each shared by two or three boys. The very sight of them was ravishing to a boy from a prep. school who had never before had a *pied-à-terre* of his own. As we were still living (culturally) in the Edwardian period, each study imitated as closely as possible the cluttered appearance of an Edwardian drawing-room; the aim was to fill the tiny cell as full as it could hold with bookcases, corner cupboards, knick-knacks, and pictures. There were two larger rooms on the same floor; one the 'Pres' Room', the synod of Olympus, and the other the New Boys' Study. It was not like a study at all. It was larger, darker, and undecorated; an immovable bench ran round a clamped table. But we knew, we ten or twelve recruits, that not all of us would be left in the New Boys' Study. Some of us would be given 'real' studies; the residue would occupy the opprobrious place for a term or so. That was the great hazard of our first evening; one was to be taken and another left.

As we sat round our clamped table, silent for the most

part and speaking in whispers when we spoke, the door would be opened at intervals; a boy would look in, smile (not at us but to himself) and withdraw. Once, over the shoulder of the smiler there came another face, and a chuckling voice said, 'Ho-ho! I know what *you're* looking for.' Only I knew what it was all about, for my brother had played Chesterfield to my Stanhope and instructed me in the manners of the Coll. None of the boys who looked in and smiled was a Blood; they were all quite young and there was something common to the faces of them all. They were, in fact, the reigning or fading Tarts of the House, trying to guess which of us were their destined rivals or successors.

It is possible that some readers will not know what a House Tart was. First, as to the adjective. All life at Wyvern was lived, so to speak, in the two concentric circles of Coll and House. You could be a Coll pre. or merely a House pre. You could be a Coll Blood or merely a House Blood, a Coll Punt (i.e., a pariah, an unpopular person) or merely a House Punt; and of course a Coll Tart or merely a House Tart. A Tart is[1] a pretty and effeminate-looking small boy who acts as a catamite to one or more of his seniors, usu-

---

[1] Here, and throughout this account, I sometimes use the 'historic present'. Heaven forfend I should be taken to mean that Wyvern is the same today.

ally Bloods. Usually, not always. Though our oligarchy kept most of the amenities of life to themselves, they were, on this point, liberal; they did not impose chastity on the middle-class boy in addition to all his other disabilities. Pederasty among the lower classes was not 'side', or at least not serious side; not like putting one's hands in one's pockets or wearing one's coat unbuttoned. The gods had a sense of proportion.

The Tarts had an important function to play in making school (what it was advertised to be) a preparation for public life. They were not like slaves, for their favours were (nearly always) solicited, not compelled. Nor were they exactly like prostitutes, for the liaison often had some permanence and, far from being merely sensual, was highly sentimentalised. Nor were they paid (in hard cash, I mean) for their services; though of course they had all the flattery, unofficial influence, favour, and privileges which the mistresses of the great have always enjoyed in adult society. That was where the Preparation for Public Life came in. It would appear from Mr Arnold Lunn's *Harrovians* that the Tarts at his school acted as informers. None of ours did. I ought to know, for one of my friends shared a study with a minor Tart; and except that he was sometimes turned out of the study when one of the Tart's lovers came in (and that, after all, was only natural) he had nothing to complain of. I was not shocked by these things. For me, at that age, the chief drawback to the whole system was that it bored me considerably. For you will have missed the atmosphere of our House unless you picture the whole place from week's end to week's end buzzing, tittering, hinting, whispering about this subject. After games, gallantry was the principal topic of polite conversation; who had 'a case with' whom, whose star was in the ascendant, who had whose photo, who and when and how often and what night and where . . . I suppose it might be called the Greek Tradition. But the vice in question is one to which I had never been tempted, and which, indeed, I still find opaque to the imagination. Possibly, if I had only stayed longer at the Coll, I might, in this respect as in others, have been turned into a Normal Boy, as the system promises. As things were, I was bored.

Those first days, like your first days in the army, were spent in a frantic endeavour to find out what you had to do. One of my first duties was to find out what 'Club' I was in. Clubs were the units to which we were assigned for compulsory games; they belonged to the Coll organisation, not the House organisation, so I had to go to a notice-board 'Up Coll' to get my facts. And first to find the place—and then to dare to squeeze oneself into the crowd of more important boys around the notice-board—

and then to begin reading through five hundred names, but always with one eye on your watch, for of course there is something else to be done within ten minutes. I was forced away from the board before I had found my name, and so, sweating, back to the House, in a flurry of anxiety, wondering how I could find time to do the job to-morrow and what unheard-of disaster might follow if I could not. (Why, by the way, do some writers talk as if care and worry were the special characteristics of adult life? It appears to me that there is more *atra cura* in an average schoolboy's week than in a grown man's average year.)

When I reached the House something gloriously unexpected happened. At the door of the Pres' Room stood one Fribble; a mere House Blood, it is true, even a minor House Blood, but to me a sufficiently exalted figure; a youth of the lean laughing type. I could hardly believe it when he actually addressed me. 'Oh, I say, Lewis,' he bawled, 'I can tell you your Club. You're in the same one as me, B6.' What a transition from all but despair to elation I underwent! All my anxiety was laid to rest. And then the graciousness of Fribble, the condescension! If a reigning monarch had asked me to dine, I could hardly have been more flattered. But there was better to follow. On every half-holiday I went dutifully to the B6 notice-board to see whether my name was down to play that afternoon or not.

And it never was. That was pure joy, for of course I hated games. My native clumsiness, combined with the lack of early training for which Belsen was responsible, had ruled out all possibility of my ever playing well enough to amuse myself, let alone to satisfy other players. I accepted games (quite a number of boys do) as one of the necessary evils of life, comparable to Income Tax or the Dentist. And so, for a week or two, I was in clover.

Then the blow fell. Fribble had lied. I was in a totally different Club. My name had more than once appeared on a notice-board I had never seen. I had committed the serious crime of 'skipping Clubs'. The punishment was a flogging administered by the Head of the Coll in the presence of the assembled Coll Pres. To the Head of the Coll himself—a red-headed, pimply boy with a name like Borage or Porridge—I can bear no grudge; it was to him a routine matter. But I must give him a name because the real point of the story requires it. The emissary (some Blood a little lower than the Head himself) who summoned me to execution attempted to reveal to me the heinousness of my crime by the words, 'Who are you? Nobody. Who is Porridge? THE MOST IMPORTANT PERSON THERE IS.'

I thought then, and I still think, that this rather missed the point. There were two perfectly good morals he could have drawn. He might have said, 'We are going to teach you never to rely on second-hand information when first-hand is available'—a very profitable lesson. Or he might have said, 'What made you think that a Blood could not be a liar?' But, 'Who are you? Nobody,' however just, seems hardly relevant. The implication is that I have skipped Club in arrogance or defiance. And I puzzle endlessly over the question whether the speaker really believed that. Did he really think it likely that an utterly helpless stranger in a new society, a society governed by an irresistible class on whose favour all his hopes of happiness depended, had set himself on the first week to pull the nose of The Most Important Person There Is? It is a problem which has met me many times in later life. What does a certain type of examiner mean when he says, 'To show up work like this is an insult to the examiners?' Does he really think that the ploughed candidate has insulted him?

Another problem is Fribble's share in my little catastrophe. Was his lie to me a hoax, a practical joke? Was he paying off some old score against my brother? Or was he (as I now think most likely) simply what our ancestors called a Rattle, a man from whose mouth information, true and false, flows out all day long without consideration, almost without volition? Some might think that, whatever his motive had originally been, he might have come forward and confessed his part when he saw what I was in for. But that, you know, was hardly to be expected. He was a very minor Blood, still climbing up the social stair; Burradge was almost as far above Fribble as Fribble was above me. By coming forward he would have imperilled his social position, in a community where social advancement was the one thing that mattered; school is a preparation for public life.

In justice to Wyvern, I must add that Fribble was not, by our standards, quite a fair representative of Bloodery. He had offended against the rules of gallantry in a manner which (my brother tells me) would have been impossible in his day. I said just now that the Tarts were solicited, not compelled. But Fribble did use all his prefectorial powers for a whole term to persecute a boy called, let us say, Parsley who had refused his suit. This was quite easy for Fribble to do. The innumerable small regulations which a junior boy could break almost unawares enabled a prefect to make sure that a given boy was nearly always in trouble, while the fagging system made it easy to see that he had no leisure at all at any hour of any day. So Parsley learned what it was to refuse even a minor Blood. The story would be more impressive if Parsley had been a virtuous boy and had refused on moral grounds. Unfortunately he was 'as common as a barber's chair', had been a reigning toast in my brother's day, and was now almost past his bloom. He drew the line at Fribble. But Fribble's attempt at coercion was the only instance of its kind I ever knew.

Indeed, taking them by and large, and considering the temptations of adolescents, so privileged, so flattered, our Bloods were not a bad lot. The Count was even kindly. The Parrot was nothing worse than a grave fool: 'Yards-of-Face' they called him. Stopfish, whom some thought cruel, even had moral principles; in his younger days many (I'm told) had desired him as a Tart, but he had kept his virtue. 'Pretty, but no good to anyone; he's *pie'* would be the Wyvernian comment. The hardest to defend, perhaps, is Tennyson. We did not much mind his being a shoplifter; some people thought it rather clever of him to come back from a tour of the town with more ties and socks than he had paid for. We minded more his favourite punishment for us rabble, 'a clip'. Yet he could truly have pleaded to the authorities that it meant merely a box on the ear. He would not have added that the patient was made to stand with his left ear, temple and cheek almost, but not quite, touching the jamb of a doorway, and then struck with full force on the right. We also grumbled a little in secret when he got up a tournament (either explicitly or virtually compulsory, I think) in a game called Yard Cricket, collected subscriptions, and neither held the tournament nor returned the cash. But you will remember that this happened in the

Marconi period, and to be a prefect is a Preparation for Public Life. And for all of them, even Tennyson, one thing can be said; they were never drunk. I was told that their predecessors, a year before I came, were sometimes very drunk indeed in the House corridor at mid-day. In fact, odd as it would have sounded to an adult, I joined the House when it was in a stern mood of moral rearmament. That was the point of a series of speeches which the prefects addressed to us all in the House Library during my first week. It was explained with a wealth of threatenings that we were to be pulled Up or Together or wherever decadents are pulled by moral reformers. Tennyson was very great on that occasion. He had a fine bass voice and sang solos in the choir. I knew one of his Tarts.

Peace to them all. A worse fate awaited them than the most vindictive fag among us could have wished. Ypres and the Somme ate up most of them. They were happy while their good days lasted.

My flogging by pimply old Ullage was no unmerciful affair in itself. The real trouble was that I think I now became, thanks to Fribble, a marked man; the sort of dangerous New Boy who skips Clubs. At least I think that must have been the main reason why I was an object of dislike to Tennyson. There were probably others. I was big for my age, a great lout of a boy, and that sets one's seniors against one. I was also useless at games. Worst of all, there was my face. I am the kind of person who gets told, 'And take that look off your face too.' Notice, once more, the mingled justice and injustice of our lives. No doubt in conceit or ill-temper I have often intended to look insolent or truculent; but on those occasions people don't appear to notice it. On the other hand, the moments at which I was told to 'take that look off' were usually those when I intended to be most abject. Can there have been a freeman somewhere among my ancestors whose expression, against my will, looked out?

As I have hinted before, the fagging system is the chief medium by which the Bloods, without breaking any rule, can make a junior boy's life a weariness to him. Different schools have different kinds of fagging. At some of them, individual Bloods have individual fags. This is the system most often depicted in school stories; it is sometimes represented as—and, for all I know, sometimes really is—a fruitful relation as of knight and squire, in which service on the one part is rewarded with some degree of countenance and protection on the other. But whatever its merits may be, we never experienced them at Wyvern. Fagging with us was as impersonal as the labour-market in Victorian England; in that way, too, the Coll was a preparation for public life. All boys under a certain seniority constituted a labour pool, the common property of all the Bloods. When a Blood wanted his OTC kit brushed and polished, or his boots cleaned, or his study 'done out', or his tea made, he shouted. We all came running, and of course the Blood gave the work to the boy he most disliked. The kit-cleaning—it took hours, and then, when you had finished it, your own kit was still to do—was the most detested *corvée.* Shoe-cleaning was a nuisance not so much in itself as in its attendant circumstances. It came at an hour which was vital for a boy like me who, having won a scholarship, had been placed in a high form and could hardly, by all his best efforts, keep up with the work. Hence the success of one's whole day in Form might depend on the precious forty minutes between breakfast and Morning School, when one went over the set passages of translation with other boys in the same Form. This could be done only if one escaped being fagged as a shoeblack. Not, of course, that it takes forty minutes to clean a pair of shoes. What takes the time is waiting in the queue of other fags in the 'boot-hole' to get your turn at the brushes and blacking. The whole look of that cellar, the darkness, the smell, and (for most of the year) the freezing cold, are a vivid memory. You must not of course suppose that, in those spacious days, we lacked servants. There were two official 'boot-boys' paid by the Housemaster for cleaning all boots and shoes, and everyone, including us fags who had cleaned both our own shoes and the Bloods' shoes daily, tipped the bootboys at the end of each term for their services.

For a reason which all English readers will understand (others will hear something of it in the next chapter) I am humiliated and embarrassed at having to record that as time went on I came to dislike the fagging system. No true defender of the Public Schools will believe me if I say that I was tired. But I was—dog-tired, cab-horse tired, tired (almost) like a child in a factory. Many things besides fagging contributed to it. I was big and had possibly outgrown my strength. My work in Form was almost beyond me. I was having a good deal of dental trouble at the time, and many nights of clamorous pain. Never, except in the front line trenches (and not always there) do I remember such aching and continuous weariness as at Wyvern. Oh, the implacable day, the horror of waking, the endless desert of hours that separated one from bed-time! And remember that, even without fagging, a schoolday contains hardly any leisure for a boy who does not like games. For him, to pass from the form-room to the playing field is simply to exchange work in which he can take some interest for work in which he can take none, in which failure is more severely punished, and in which (worst of all) he must feign an interest.

I think that this feigning, this ceaseless pretence of interest in matters to me supremely boring, was what wore
me out more than anything else. If the reader will picture himself, unarmed, shut up for thirteen weeks on end,
night and day, in a society of fanatical golfers—or, if he is a
golfer himself, let him substitute fishermen, theosophists,
bimetallists, Baconians, or German undergraduates with
a taste for autobiography—who all carry revolvers and
will probably shoot him if he ever seems to lose interest in
their conversation, he will have an idea of my school life.
Even the hardy Chowbok (in *Erewhon*) quailed at such a
destiny. For games (and gallantry) were the only subjects,
and I cared for neither. But I must seem to care for both,
for a boy goes to a Public School precisely to be made a
normal, sensible boy—a good mixer—to be taken out of
himself; and eccentricity is severely penalised.

You must not, from this, hastily conclude that most boys
liked *playing* games any better than I did. To escape Clubs
was considered by dozens of boys an obvious good. Leave
off Clubs required the Housemaster's signature, and that
harmless Merovingian's signature was imitable. A com-
petent forger (I knew one member of the profession) by
manufacturing and selling forged signatures could make
a steady addition to his pocket money. The perpetual
talk about games depended on three things. First, on the

same sort of genuine (though hardly practical) enthusiasm which sends the crowds to the League Football Matches. Few wanted to play, but many wanted to watch, to participate vicariously in the triumphs of the Coll, or the House, team. Secondly, this natural feeling had the vigilant backing of all the Bloods and nearly all the Masters. To be lukewarm on such matters was the supreme sin. Hence enthusiasm had to be exaggerated where it existed and simulated where it did not. At cricket matches minor Bloods patrolled the crowd of spectators to detect and punish any 'slackness' in the applause; it reminds one of the precautions taken when Nero sang. For of course the whole structure of Bloodery would collapse if the Bloods played in the spirit of play, for their recreation; there must be audience and limelight. And this brings us to the third reason. For boys who were not yet Bloods but who had some athletic promise, Games were essentially a *moyen de parvenir.* There was nothing recreational about Clubs for them any more than for me. They went to the playing fields not as men go to the tennis-club but as stage-struck girls go to an Audition; tense and anxious, racked with dazzling hopes and sickening fears, never in peace of mind till they had won some notice which would set their feet on the first rung of the social ladder. And not then at peace either; for not to advance is to fall back.

The truth is that organised and compulsory games had, in my day, banished the element of play from school life almost entirely. There was no time to play (in the proper sense of the word). The rivalry was too fierce, the prizes too glittering, the 'hell of failure' too severe.

The only boy, almost, who 'played' (but not at games) was our Irish earl. But then he was an exception to all rules; not because of his earldom but because he was an untamable Irishman, anarch in grain, whom no society could iron out. He smoked a pipe in his first term. He went off by night on strange expeditions to a neighbouring city; not, I believe, for women, but for harmless rowdyism, low life, and adventure. He always carried a revolver. I remember it well, for he had a habit of loading one chamber only, rushing into your study, and then firing off (if that is the right word) all the others at you, so that your life depended on his counting accurately. I felt at the time, and I feel still, that this (unlike the fagging) was the sort of thing no sensible boy could object to. It was done in defiance both of masters and Bloods, it was wholly useless, and there was no malice in it. I liked Ballygunnian; he, too, was killed in France. I do not think he ever became a Blood; if he had, he wouldn't have noticed it. He cared nothing for the limelight or for social success. He passed through the Coll without paying it any attention.

I suppose Popsy—the pretty red-head who was house-maid on 'the Private side'—might also rank as an element making for 'play'. Popsy, when caught and carried bodily into our part of the House (I think by the Count), was all giggles and screams. She was too sensible a girl to sur-render her 'virtue' to any Blood; but it was rumoured that those who found her in the right time and place might induce her to give certain lessons in anatomy. Perhaps they lied.

I have hardly mentioned a Master yet. One master, dearly loved and reverenced, will appear in the next chap-ter. But other masters are hardly worth speaking of. It is difficult for parents (and more difficult, perhaps, for schoolmasters) to realise the unimportance of most mas-ters in the life of a school. Of the good and evil which is done to a schoolboy masters, in general, do little, and know less. Our own Housemaster must have been an upright man, for he fed us excellently. For the rest, he treated his House in a very gentlemanly, uninquisi-tive way. He sometimes walked round the dormitories of a night, but he always wore boots, trod heavily and coughed at the door. He was no spy and no kill-joy, hon-est man. Live and let live.

As I grew more and more tired, both in body and mind, I came to hate Wyvern. I did not notice the real harm it was doing to me. It was gradually teaching me to be a prig; that is, an intellectual prig or (in the bad sense) a High Brow. But that subject must wait for another chapter. At the tail-end of this I must repeat (for this is the overall impression left by Wyvern) that I was tired. Consciousness itself was becoming the supreme evil; sleep, the prime good. To lie down, to be out of the sound of voices, to pretend and grimace and evade and slink no more, that was the object of all desire—if only there were not another morning ahead—if only sleep could last for ever!

VII

LIGHT AND SHADE

No situation, however wretched it seems, but has
some sort of comfort attending it.

GOLDSMITH

Here's a fellow, you say, who used to come before us as a
moral and religious writer, and now, if you please, he's
written a whole chapter describing his old school as a furnace of impure loves without one word on the heinousness
of the sin. But there are two reasons. One you shall hear
before this chapter ends. The other is that, as I have said,
the sin in question is one of the two (gambling is the other)
which I have never been tempted to commit. I will not
indulge in futile philippics against enemies I never met in
battle.

('This means, then, that all the other vices you have so
largely written about . . .' Well, yes, it does, and more's the
pity; but it's nothing to our purpose at the moment.)

I have now to tell you how Wyvern made me a prig.

When I went there, nothing was farther from my mind than the idea that my private taste for fairly good books, for Wagner, for mythology, gave me any sort of superiority to those who read nothing but magazines and listened to nothing but the (then fashionable) Rag-time. The claim might seem unbelievable if I did not add that I had been protected from this sort of conceit by downright ignorance. Mr Ian Hay somewhere draws a picture of the reading minority at a Public School in his day as boys who talked about 'GBS and GKC' in the same spirit in which other boys secretly smoked; both sets were inspired by the same craving for forbidden fruit and the same desire to be grown-up. And I suppose boys such as he describes might come from Chelsea or Oxford or Cambridge homes where they heard things about contemporary literature. But my position was wholly different. I was, for example, a great reader of Shaw about the time I went to Wyvern, but I had never dreamed that reading Shaw was anything to be proud of. Shaw was an author on my father's shelves like any other author. I began reading him because his *Dramatic Opinions* contained a good deal about Wagner and Wagner's very name was then a lure to me. Thence I went on to read most of the other Shaws we had. But how his reputation stood in the literary world I neither knew nor cared; I didn't know there was 'a literary world'. My father told me Shaw was 'a mountebank' but that there were some laughs in *John Bull's Other Island.* It was the same with all my other reading; no one (thank God) had ever admired or encouraged it. (William Morris, for some unfathomable reason, my father always referred to as 'that whistlepainter'.) I might be—no doubt I was—conceited at Chartres for being good at my Latin; this was something recognised as meritorious. But 'Eng. Lit.' was blessedly absent from the official syllabus, so I was saved from any possibility of conceit about it. Never in my life had I read a work of fiction, poetry, or criticism in my own language except because, after trying the first few pages, I liked the taste of it. I could not help knowing that most other people, boys and grown-ups alike, did not care for the books I read. A very few tastes I could share with my father, a few more with my brother; apart from that, there was no point of contact, and this I accepted as a sort of natural law. If I reflected on it at all, it would have given me, I think, a slight feeling, not of superiority, but of inferiority. The latest popular novel was so obviously a more adult, a more normal, a more sophisticated taste than any of mine. A certain shame or bashfulness attached itself to whatever one deeply and privately enjoyed. I went to the Coll far more disposed to excuse my literary tastes than to plume myself on them.

But this innocence did not last. I was, from the first, a little shaken by all that I soon began to learn from my form-master about the glories of literature. I was at last made free of the dangerous secret that others had, like me, found there 'enormous bliss' and been maddened by beauty. Among the other New Bugs of my year, too, I met a pair of boys who came from the Dragon School at Oxford (where Naomi Mitchison in her teens had just produced her first play) and from them also I got the dim impression that there was a world I had never dreamed of, a world in which poetry, say, was a thing public and accepted, just as Games and Gallantry were accepted at Wyvern; nay, a world in which a taste for such things was almost meritorious. I felt as Siegfried felt when it first dawned on him that he was not Mime's son. What had been 'my' taste was apparently 'our' taste (if only I could ever meet the 'we' to whom that 'our' belonged). And if 'our' taste, then—by a perilous transition—perhaps 'good' taste or 'the right taste'. For that transition involves a kind of Fall. The moment good taste knows itself, some of its goodness is lost. Even then, however, it is not necessary to take the further downward step of despising the 'philistines' who do not share it. Unfortunately I took it. Hitherto, though increasingly miserable at Wyvern, I had been half ashamed of my own misery, still ready (if I were only allowed) to admire the Olympians, still a little overawed, cowed rather than resentful. I had, you see, no standing place against the Wyvernian *ethos,* no side for which I could play against it; it was a bare 'I' against what seemed simply the world. But the moment that 'I' became, however vaguely, a *we*—and Wyvern not *the* world but *a* world—the whole thing changed. It was now possible, at least in thought, to retaliate. I can remember what may well have been the precise moment of this transition. A prefect called Blugg or Glubb or some such name stood opposite me, belching in my face, giving me some order. The belching was not intended as an insult. You can't 'insult' a fag any more than an animal. If Bulb had thought of my reactions at all, he would have expected me to find his eructations funny. What pushed me over the edge into pure priggery was his face—the puffy bloated cheeks, the thick, moist, sagging lower lip, the yokel blend of drowsiness and cunning. 'The lout!' I thought. 'The clod! The dull, crass clown! For all his powers and privileges, I would not be he.' I had become a Prig, a High-Brow.

The interesting thing is that the Public School system had thus produced the very thing which it was advertised to prevent or cure. For you must understand (if you have not been dipped in that tradition yourself) that the whole thing was devised to 'knock the nonsense' out of the smaller boys and 'put them in their place'. 'If the junior boys weren't fagged,' as my brother once said, 'they would become unsufferable.' That is why I felt so embarrassed, a few pages ago, when I had to confess that I got rather tired of perpetual fagging. If you say this, every true defender of the system will diagnose your case at once, and they will all diagnose it in the same way. 'Hoho!' they will cry, 'so *that's* the trouble! Thought yourself too good to black your betters' boots, did you? That just shows how badly you needed to be fagged. It's to cure young prigs like you that the system exists.' That any cause except 'thinking yourself too good for it' might awaken discontent with a fag's lot will not be admitted. You have only to transfer the thing to adult life and you will, apparently, see the full logic of the position. If some neighbouring VIP had irresistible authority to call on you for any service he pleased at any hour when you were not in the office—if, when you came home on a summer evening, tired from work and with more work to prepare against the morrow, he could drag you to the links and make you his caddy till the light failed—if at last he dismissed you unthanked with a suitcase full of his clothes to brush and clean and return to him before breakfast, and a hamper full of his foul linen for your wife to wash and mend—and if, under this regime, you were not always perfectly happy and contented; where could the cause lie except in your own vanity? What else, after all, could it be? For, almost by definition, every offence a junior boy commits must be due to 'cheek' or 'side'; and to be miserable, even to fall short of rapturous enthusiasm, is an offence.

Obviously a certain grave danger was ever-present to the minds of those who built up the Wyvernian hierarchy. It seemed to them self-evident that, if you left things to themselves, boys of nineteen who played rugger for the county and boxed for the school would everywhere be knocked down and sat on by boys of thirteen. And that, you know, would be a very shocking spectacle. The most elaborate mechanism, therefore, had to be devised for protecting the strong against the weak, the close corporation of Old Hands against the parcel of newcomers who were strangers to one another and to everyone in the place, the poor, trembling lions against the furious and ravening sheep.

There is, of course, some truth in it. Small boys can be cheeky; and half an hour in the society of a French thirteen-year-old makes most of us feel that there is something to be said for fagging after all. Yet I cannot help thinking that the bigger boys would have been able to hold their own without all the complicated assurances, pattings on the back, and encouragement which the authorities gave them. For, of course, these authorities, not content with knocking the 'nonsense' out of the sheep, were always coaxing and petting an at least equal quantity of 'nonsense' into the lions; power and privilege and an applauding audience for the games they play. Might not the mere nature of boys have done all, and rather more than all, that needed doing in this direction without assistance?

But whatever the rationality of the design, I contend that it did not achieve its object. For the last thirty years or so England has been filled with a bitter, truculent, sceptical, debunking, and cynical *intelligentsia*. A great many of them were at public schools, and I believe very few of them liked it. Those who defend the schools will, of course, say that these Prigs are the cases which the system failed to cure; they were not kicked, mocked, fagged, flogged, and humiliated enough. But surely it is equally possible that they are the products of the system? That they were not Prigs at all when they came to their schools but were made Prigs by their first year, as I was? For, really, that would be a very natural result. Where oppression does not completely and permanently break the spirit, has it not a natural tendency to produce retaliatory pride and contempt? We reimburse ourselves for cuffs and toil by a double dose of self-esteem. No one is more likely to be arrogant than a lately freed slave.

I write, of course, only to neutral readers. With the whole-hearted adherents of the system there is no arguing, for, as we have already seen, they have maxims and logic which the lay mind cannot apprehend. I have even heard them defend compulsory games on the ground that all boys 'except a few rotters' like the games; they have to be compulsory because no compulsion is needed. (I wish I had never heard chaplains in the Armed Forces produce a similar argument in defence of the wicked institution of Church Parades.)

But the essential evil of public school life, as I see it, did not lie either in the sufferings of the fags or in the privileged arrogance of the Bloods. These were symptoms of something more all-persuasive, something which, in the long run, did most harm to the boys who succeeded best at school and were happiest there. Spiritually speaking, the deadly thing was that school life was a life almost wholly dominated by the social struggle; to get on, to arrive, or, having reached the top, to remain there, was the absorbing preoccupation. It is often, of course, the preoccupation of adult life as well; but I have not yet seen any adult society in which the surrender to this impulse was so total. And from it, at school as in the world, all sorts of meanness flow; the sycophancy that courts those higher in the scale, the cultivation of those whom it is well to know, the speedy abandonment of friendships that will not help on the upward path, the readiness to join the cry against the unpopular, the secret motive in almost every action. The Wyvernians seem to me in retrospect to have been the least spontaneous, in that sense the least boyish, society I have ever known. It would perhaps not be too much to say that in some boys' lives everything was calculated to the great end of advancement. For this games were played; for this clothes, friends, amusements, and vices were chosen.

And that is why I cannot give pederasty anything like a first place among the evils of the Coll. There is much hypocrisy on this theme. People commonly talk as if every other evil were more tolerable than this. But why? Because those of us who do not share the vice feel for it a certain nausea, as we do, say, for necrophily? I think that of very little relevance to moral judgement. Because it produces permanent perversion? But there is very little evidence that it does. The Bloods would have preferred girls to boys if they could have come by them; when, at a later age, girls were obtainable, they probably took them. Is it then on Christian grounds? But how many of those who fulminate on the matter are in fact Christians? And what Christian in a society so worldly and cruel as that of Wyvern, would pick out the carnal sins for special reprobation? Cruelty is surely more evil than lust and the

World at least as dangerous as the Flesh. The real reason for all the pother is, in my opinion, neither Christian nor ethical. We attack this vice not because it is the worst but because it is, by adult standards, the most disreputable and unmentionable, and happens also to be a crime in English law. The World will lead you only to Hell; but sodomy may lead you to jail and create a scandal, and lose you your job. The World, to do it justice, seldom does that.

If those of us who have known a school like Wyvern dared to speak the truth, we should have to say that pederasty, however great an evil in itself, was, in that time and place, the only foothold or cranny left for certain good things. It was the only counterpoise to the social struggle; the one oasis (though green only with weeds and moist only with foetid water) in the burning desert of competitive ambition. In his unnatural love-affairs, and perhaps only there, the Blood went a little out of himself, forgot for a few hours that he was One of the Most Important People There Are. It softens the picture. A perversion was the only chink left through which something spontaneous and uncalculating could creep in. Plato was right after all. Eros, turned upside down, blackened, distorted, and filthy, still bore traces of his divinity.

What an answer, by the by, Wyvern was to those who derive all the ills of society from economics! For money had nothing to do with its class system. It was not (thank Heaven) the boys with threadbare coats who became Punts, nor the boys with plenty of pocket-money who became Bloods. According to some theorists, therefore, it ought to have been entirely free from bourgeois vulgarities and iniquities. Yet I have never seen a community so competitive, so full of snobbery and flunkeyism, a ruling class so selfish and so class-conscious, or a proletariat so fawning, so lacking in all solidarity and sense of corporate honour. But perhaps one hardly needs to cite experience for a truth so obvious *a priori*. As Aristotle remarked, men do not become dictators in order to keep warm. If a ruling class has some other source of strength, why need it bother about money? Most of what it wants will be pressed upon it by emulous flatterers; the rest can be taken by force.

There were two blessings at Wyvern that wore no disguise; one of them was my form master, Smewgy as we called him. I spell the name so as to insure the right pronunciation—the first syllable should rhyme exactly with *Fugue*—though the Wyvernian spelling was 'Smugy'.

Except at Oldie's I had been fortunate in my teachers ever since I was born; but Smewgy was 'beyond expectation, beyond hope'. He was a grey-head with large spectacles and a wide mouth which combined to give him a froglike expression, but nothing could be less froglike than his voice. He was honey-tongued. Every verse he read turned into music on his lips: something midway between speech and song. It is not the only good way of reading verse, but it is the way to enchant boys; more dramatic and less rhythmical ways can be learned later. He first taught me the right sensuality of poetry, how it should be savoured and mouthed in solitude. Of Milton's 'Thrones, Dominations, Princedoms, Virtues, Powers' he said, 'That line made me happy for a week.' It was not the sort of thing I had heard anyone say before. Nor had I ever met before perfect courtesy in a teacher. It had nothing to do with softness; Smewgy could be very severe, but it was the severity of a judge, weighty and measured, without taunting—

He never yet no vileinye ne sayde
In all his lyf unto no maner wight.

He had a difficult team to drive, for our form consisted partly of youngsters, New Bugs with scholarships, starting there like myself, and partly of veterans who had arrived there at the end of their slow journey up the school. He made us a unity by his good manners. He always addressed us as 'gentlemen' and the possibility of behaving otherwise seemed thus to be ruled out from the beginning; and in that room at least the distinction between fags and Bloods never raised its head. On a hot day, when he had given us permission to remove our coats, he asked our permission before removing his gown. Once for bad work I was sent by him to the Headmaster to be threatened and rated. The Headmaster misunderstood Smewgy's report and thought there had been some complaint about my manners. Afterward Smewgy got wind of the Head's actual words and at once corrected the mistake, drawing me aside and saying, 'There has been some curious misunderstanding. I said nothing of the sort about you. You will have to be whipped if you don't do better at your Greek Grammar next week, but naturally that has nothing to do with your manners or mine.' The idea that the tone of conversation between one gentleman and another should be altered by a flogging (any more than by a duel) was ridiculous. His manner was perfect: no familiarity, no hostility, no threadbare humour; mutual respect; decorum. 'Never let us live with *amousia*,' was one of his favourite maxims: *amousia*, the absence of the Muses. And he knew, as Spenser knew, that courtesy was of the Muses.

Thus, even had he taught us nothing else, to be in Smewgy's form was to be in a measure ennobled. Amidst all the banal ambition and flashy splendours of school life he stood as a permanent reminder of things more gracious, more humane, larger and cooler. But his teaching, in the narrower sense, was equally good. He could enchant but he could also analyse. An idiom or a textual crux, once expounded by Smewgy, became clear as day. He made us feel that the scholar's demand for accuracy was not merely pedantic, still less an arbitrary moral discipline, but rather a niceness, a delicacy, to lack which argued 'a gross and swainish disposition.' I began to see that the reader who misses syntactical points in a poem is missing aesthetic points as well.

In those days a boy on the classical side officially did almost nothing but classics. I think this was wise; the greatest service we can do to education today is to teach fewer subjects. No one has time to do more than a very few things well before he is twenty, and when we force a boy to be a mediocrity in a dozen subjects we destroy his standards, perhaps for life. Smewgy taught us Latin and Greek, but everything else came in incidentally. The books I liked best under his teaching were Horace's Odes, Aeneid IV, and Euripides' *Bacchae*. I had always in one sense 'liked' my classical work, but hitherto this had only been the pleasure that everyone feels in mastering a craft. Now I tasted the classics as poetry. Euripides' picture of Dionysus was closely linked in my mind with the whole mood of Mr Stephens' *Crock of Gold*, which I had lately read for the first time with great excitement. Here was something very different from the Northernness. Pan and Dionysus lacked the cold, piercing appeal of Odin and Frey. A new quality entered my imagination: something Mediterranean and volcanic, the orgiastic drum beat. Orgiastic, but not, or not strongly, erotic. It was perhaps unconsciously connected with my growing hatred of the public school orthodoxies and conventions, my desire to break and tear it all.

The other undisguised blessing of the Coll was 'the Gurney,' the school library; not only because it was a library, but because it was a sanctuary. As the Negro used to become free on touching English soil, so the meanest boy was 'unfaggable' once he was inside the Gurney. It was not, of course, easy to get there. In the winter terms if you were not on the list for 'Clubs' you had to go out for a run. In summer you could reach sanctuary of an afternoon only under favourable conditions. You might be put down for Clubs, and that excluded you. Or there might be either a House match or a Coll match which you were compelled to watch. Thirdly, and most probably, on your way to the Gurney you might be caught and fagged for the whole afternoon. But sometimes one succeeded in running the gauntlet of all these dangers; and then—the books, silence, leisure, the distant sound of bat and ball ('oh the brave music of a *distant* drum'), bees buzzing at the open windows, and freedom. In the Gurney I found *Corpus Poeticum Boreale* and tried, vainly but happily, to hammer out the originals from the translation at the bottom of the page. There too I found Milton, and Yeats, and a book on Celtic mythology, which soon became, if not a rival, yet a humble companion, to Norse. That did me good; to enjoy two mythologies (or three, now that I had begun to love the Greek), fully aware of their differing flavours, is a balancing thing, and makes for catholicity. I felt keenly the difference between the stony and fiery sublimity of Asgard, the green, leafy, amorous, and elusive world of Cruachan and the Red Branch and Tir-nan-Og, the harder, more defiant, sun-bright beauty of Olympus. I began (presumably in the holidays) an epic on Cuchulain and another on Finn, in English hexameters and in fourteeners respectively. Luckily they were abandoned before these easy and vulgar metres had time to spoil my ear.

But the Northernness still came first and the only work I completed at this time was a tragedy, Norse in subject and Greek in form. It was called *Loki Bound* and was as classical as any Humanist could have desired, with Prologos, Parodos, Epeisodia, Stasima, Exodos, Stichomythia, and (of course) one passage in trochaic *septenarii*—with rhyme.

I never enjoyed anything more. The content is significant. My Loki was not merely malicious. He was against Odin because Odin had created a world though Loki had clearly warned him that this was a wanton cruelty. Why should creatures have the burden of existence forced on them without their consent? The main contrast in my play was between the sad wisdom of Loki and the brutal orthodoxy of Thor. Odin was partly sympathetic; he could at least see what Loki meant and there had been old friendship between those two before cosmic politics forced them apart. Thor was the real villain, Thor with his hammer and his threats, who was always egging Odin on against Loki and always complaining that Loki did not sufficiently respect the major gods; to which Loki replied

I pay respect to wisdom not to strength.

Thor was, in fact, the symbol of the Bloods; though I see that more clearly now than I did at the time. Loki was a projection of myself; he voiced that sense of priggish superiority whereby I was, unfortunately, beginning to compensate myself for my unhappiness.

The other feature in *Loki Bound* which may be worth commenting on is the pessimism. I was at this time living, like so many Atheists or Antitheists, in a whirl of contradictions. I maintained that God did not exist. I was also very angry with God for not existing. I was equally angry with Him for creating a world.

How far was this pessimism, this desire not to have been, sincere? Well, I must confess that this desire quite slipped out of my mind during the seconds when I was covered by the wild Earl's revolver. By the Chestertonian test, then, the test of *Manalive*, it was not sincere at all. But I am still not convinced by Chesterton's argument. It is true that when a pessimist's life is threatened he behaves like other men; his impulse to preserve life is stronger than his judgement that life is not worth preserving. But how does this prove that the judgement was insincere or even erroneous? A man's judgement that whisky is bad for him is not invalidated by the fact that when the bottle is at hand he finds desire stronger than reason and succumbs. Having once tasted life, we are subjected to the impulse of self-preservation. Life, in other words, is as habit-forming as cocaine. What then? If I still held creation to be 'a great injustice' I should hold that this impulse to retain life aggravates the injustice. If it is bad to be forced to drink the potion, how does it mend matters that the potion turns out to be an addiction drug? Pessimism cannot be answered so. Thinking as I then thought about the universe, I was reasonable in condemning it. At the same time

I now see that my view was closely connected with a certain lopsidedness of temperament. I had always been more violent in my negative than in my positive demands. Thus in personal relations, I could forgive much neglect more easily than the least degree of what I regarded as interference. At table I could forgive much insipidity in my food more easily than the least suspicion of what seemed to me excessive or inappropriate seasoning. In the course of life I could put up with any amount of monotony far more patiently than even the smallest disturbance, bother, bustle, or what the Scotch call *kerfuffle*. Never at any age did I clamour to be amused; always and at all ages (where I dared) I hotly demanded not to be interrupted. The pessimism, or cowardice, which would prefer nonexistence itself to even the mildest unhappiness was thus merely the generalisation of all these pusillanimous preferences. And it remains true that I have, almost all my life, been quite unable to feel that horror of nonentity, of annihilation, which, say, Dr Johnson felt so strongly. I felt it for the first time only in 1947. But that was after I had long been reconverted and thus begun to know what life really is and what would have been lost by missing it.

VIII

RELEASE

As Fortune is wont, at her chosen hour,
Whether she sends us solace or sore,
The wight to whom she shows her power
Will find that he gets still more and more.

PEARL

A few chapters ago I warned the reader that the return of
Joy had introduced into my life a duality which makes it
difficult to narrate. Reading through what I have just written about Wyvern, I find myself exclaiming, 'Lies, lies!
This was really a period of ecstasy. It consisted chiefly of
moments when you were too happy to speak, when the
gods and heroes rioted through your head, when satyrs
danced and Maenads roared on the mountains, when
Brynhild and Sieglinde, Deirdre, Maeve and Helen were all
about you, till sometimes you felt that it might break you
with mere richness.' And all that is true. There were more
Leprechauns than fags in that House. I have seen the victo-

ries of Cuchulain more often than those of the first eleven. Was Borage the Head of the Coll? or was it Conachar MacNessa? And the world itself—can I have been unhappy, living in Paradise? What keen, tingling sunlight there was! The mere smells were enough to make a man tipsy—cut grass, dew-dabbled mosses, sweet pea, autumn woods, wood burning, peat, salt water. The sense ached. I was sick with desire; that sickness better than health. All this is true, but it does not make the other version a lie. I am telling a story of two lives. They had nothing to do with each other: oil and vinegar, a river running beside a canal, Jekyll and Hyde. Fix your eye on either and it claims to be the sole truth. When I remember my outer life I see clearly that the other is but momentary flashes, seconds of gold scattered in months of dross, each instantly swallowed up in the old, familiar, sordid, hopeless weariness. When I remember my inner life I see that everything mentioned in the last two chapters was merely a coarse curtain which at any moment might be drawn aside to reveal all the heavens I then knew. The same duality perplexes the story of my home life, to which I must now turn.

Once my brother had left Wyvern and I had gone to it, the classic period of our boyhood was at an end. Something not so good succeeded it, but this had long been prepared by slow development within the classic age itself. All began, as I have said, with the fact that our father was out of the house from nine in the morning till six at night. From the very first we built up for ourselves a life that excluded him. He on his part demanded a confidence even more boundless, perhaps, than a father usually, or wisely, demands. One instance of this, early in my life, had far reaching effects. Once when I was at Oldie's and had just begun to try to live as a Christian I wrote out a set of rules for myself and put them in my pocket. On the first day of the holidays, noticing that my pockets bulged with all sorts of papers and that my coat was being pulled out of all shape, he plucked out the whole pile of rubbish and began to go through it. Boylike, I would have died rather than let him see my list of good resolutions. I managed to keep them out of his reach and get them into the fire. I do not see that either of us was to blame; but never from that moment until the hour of his death did I enter his house without first going through my own pockets and removing anything that I wished to keep private.

A habit of concealment was thus bred before I had anything guilty to conceal. By now I had plenty. And even what I had no wish to hide I could not tell. To have told him what Wyvern or even Chartres was really like would have been risky (he might write to the Headmaster) and intolerably embarrassing. It would also have been impossible, and here I must touch on one of his strangest characteristics.

My father—but these words, at the head of a paragraph, will carry the reader's mind inevitably to *Tristram Shandy*. On second thoughts I am content that they should. It is only in a Shandean spirit that my matter can be approached. I have to describe something as odd and whimsical as ever entered the brain of Sterne; and if I could, I would gladly lead you to the same affection for my father as you have for Tristram's. And now for the thing itself. You will have grasped that my father was no fool. He had even a streak of genius in him. At the same time he had—when seated in his own armchair after a heavy mid-day dinner on an August afternoon with all the windows shut—more power of confusing an issue or taking up a fact wrongly than any man I have ever known. As a result it was impossible to drive into his head any of the realities of our school life, after which (nevertheless) he repeatedly enquired. The first and simplest barrier to communication was that, having earnestly asked, he did not 'stay for an answer' or forgot it the moment it was uttered. Some facts must have been asked for and told him on a moderate computation, once a week, and were received by him each time as perfect novelties. But this was the simplest barrier. Far more often he retained something, but something very unlike what you

had said. His mind so bubbled over with humour, sentiment, and indignation that, long before he had understood
or even listened to your words, some accidental hint had
set his imagination to work, he had produced his own version of the facts, and believed that he was getting it from
you. As he invariably got proper names wrong (no name
seemed to him less probable than another) his *textus recep-
tus* was often almost unrecognisable. Tell him that a boy
called Churchwood had caught a fieldmouse and kept it as
a pet, and a year, or ten years later, he would ask you, 'Did
you ever hear what became of poor Chickweed who was
so afraid of the rats?' For his own version, once adopted,
was indelible, and attempts to correct it only produced
an incredulous 'Hm! Well, that's not the story you *used*
to tell.' Sometimes, indeed, he took in the facts you had
stated; but truth fared none the better for that. What are
facts without interpretation? It was axiomatic to my father
(in theory) that nothing was said or done from an obvious motive. Hence he who in his real life was the most
honourable and impulsive of men, and the easiest victim
that any knave or imposter could hope to meet, became a
positive Machiavel when he knitted his brows and applied
to the behaviour of people he had never seen the spec-
tral and labyrinthine operation which he called 'reading
between the lines'. Once embarked upon that, he might

make his landfall anywhere in the wide world: and always with unshakable conviction. 'I see it all'—'I understand it perfectly'—'It's as plain as a pikestaff,' he would say; and then, as we soon learned, he would believe till his dying day in some deadly quarrel, some slight, some secret sorrow or some immensely complex machination, which was not only improbable but impossible. Dissent on our part was attributed, with kindly laughter, to our innocence, gullibility, and general ignorance of life. And besides all these confusions, there were the sheer *non sequiturs* when the ground seemed to open at one's feet. 'Did Shakespeare spell his name with an E at the end?' asked my brother. 'I believe,' said I—but my father interrupted: 'I very much doubt if he used the Italian calligraphy *at all.*' A certain church in Belfast has both a Greek inscription over the door and a curious tower. 'That church is a great landmark,' said I, 'I can pick it out from all sorts of places—even from the top of Cave Hill.' 'Such nonsense,' said my father, 'how could you make out Greek letters three or four miles away?'

One conversation, held several years later, may be recorded as a specimen of these continual cross-purposes. My brother had been speaking of a reunion dinner for the officers of the Nth Division which he had lately attended. 'I suppose your friend Collins was there,' said my father.

B. Collins? Oh no. He wasn't in the Nth, you know.

F. (After a pause.) Did these fellows not like Collins then?

B. I don't quite understand. What fellows?

F. The Johnnies that got up the dinner.

B. Oh no, not at all. It was nothing to do with liking or not liking. You see, it was a purely Divisional affair. There'd be no question of asking anyone who hadn't been in the Nth.

F. (After a long pause.) Hm! Well, I'm sure poor Collins was very much hurt.

There are situations in which the very genius of Filial Piety would find it difficult not to let some sign of impatience escape him.

I would not commit the sin of Ham. Nor would I, as historian, reduce a complex character to a false simplicity. The man who, in his armchair, sometimes appeared not so much incapable of understanding anything as determined to misunderstand everything, was formidable in the police court and, I presume, efficient in his office. He was a humorist, even, on occasion, a wit. When he was dying, the pretty nurse, rallying him, said, 'What an old pessimist you are! You're just like my father.' 'I suppose,' replied her patient, 'he has *several* daughters.'

The hours my father spent at home were thus hours of perplexity for us boys. After an evening of the sort of conversation I have been describing one felt as if one's head were spinning like a top. His presence put an end to all our innocent as well as to all our forbidden occupations. It is a hard thing—nay, a wicked thing—when a man is felt to be an intruder in his own house. And yet, as Johnson said, 'Sensation is sensation.' I am sure it was not his fault, I believe much of it was ours; what is certain is that I increasingly found it oppressive to be with him. One of his most amiable qualities helped to make it so. I have said before that he 'conned no state'; except during his Philippics he treated us as equals. The theory was that we lived together more like three brothers than like a father and two sons. That, I say, was the theory. But of course it was not and could not be so; indeed ought not to have been so. That relation cannot really exist between schoolboys and a middle-aged man of overwhelming personality and of habits utterly unlike theirs. And the pretence that it does ends by putting a curious strain on the juniors. Chesterton has laid his finger on the weak point of all such factitious equality: 'If a boy's aunts are his pals, will it not soon follow that a boy needs no pals but his aunts?' That was not, of course, the question for us; we wanted no pals. But we did want liberty, if only liberty

to walk about the house. And my father's theory that we
were three boys together actually meant that while he was
at home we were as closely bound to his presence as if the
three of us had been chained together; and all our habits
were frustrated. Thus if my father came home unexpect-
edly at mid-day, having allowed himself an extra half-
holiday, he might, if it were summer, find us with chairs
and books in the garden. An austere parent, of the formal
school, would have gone in to his own adult occupations.
Not so my father. Sitting in the garden? An excellent idea.
But would not all three of us be better on the summer-
seat? Thither, after he had assumed one of his 'light spring
overcoats', we would go. (I do not know how many overcoats he had; I am still wearing two of them.) After sitting
for a few minutes, thus clad, on a shadeless seat where the
noon-day sun was blistering the paint, he not unnaturally
began to perspire. 'I don't know what you two think,'
he would say, 'but I'm finding this almost *too* hot. What
about moving indoors?' That meant an adjournment to
the study, where even the smallest chink of open window
was rather grudgingly allowed. I say 'allowed', but there
was no question of authority. In theory, everything was
decided by the general Will. 'Liberty Hall, boys, Liberty
Hall,' as he delighted to quote. 'What time would you
like lunch?' But we knew only too well that the meal

which would otherwise have been at one had already been shifted, in obedience to his lifelong preference, to two or even two-thirty; and that the cold meats which we liked had already been withdrawn in favour of the only food our father ever voluntarily ate—hot butcher's meat, boiled, stewed or roast . . . and this to be eaten in mid-afternoon in a dining-room that faced south. For the whole of the rest of the day, whether sitting or walking, we were inseparable; and the speech (you see that it could hardly be called conversation), the speech with its cross-purposes, with its tone (inevitably) always set by him, continued intermittently till bedtime. I should be worse than a dog if I blamed my lonely father for thus desiring the friendship of his sons; or even if the miserable return I made him did not to this day lie heavy on my conscience. But 'sensation is sensation'. It was extraordinarily tiring. And in my own contributions to these endless talks—which were indeed too adult for me, too anecdotal, too prevailingly jocular—I was increasingly aware of an artificiality. The anecdotes were, indeed, admirable in their kind: business stories, Mahaffy stories (many of which I found attached to Jowett at Oxford), stories of ingenious swindles, social blunders, police-court 'drunks'. But I was acting when I responded to them. Drollery, whimsicality, the kind of humour that borders on the fantastic, was my line. I had to act. My father's geniality and my own furtive disobediences both helped to drive me into hypocrisy. I could not 'be myself' while he was at home. God forgive me, I thought Monday morning, when he went back to his work, the brightest jewel in the week.

Such was the situation which developed during the classic period. Now, when I had gone to Wyvern and my brother to a tutor to prepare for Sandhurst, there came a change. My brother had liked Wyvern as much as I loathed it. There were many reasons for this: his more adaptable temper, his face which bore no such smack-inviting signature as mine, but most of all the fact that he had gone there straight from Oldie's and I from a pre-paratory school where I had been happy. No school in England but would have appeared a heaven on earth after Oldie's. Thus in one of his first letters from Wyvern my brother communicated the startling fact that you could really eat as much (or as little) as you wanted at table. To a boy fresh from the school at Belsen, this alone would have outweighed almost everything else. But by the time I went to Wyvern I had learned to take decent feeding for granted. And now a terrible thing happened. My reaction to Wyvern was perhaps the first great disappointment my brother had ever experienced. Loving the place as he did, he had looked forward to the days when this too could be shared between us—an *idem sentire* about Wyvern succeeding an *idem sentire* about Boxen. Instead he heard, from me, blasphemies against all his gods; from Wyvern, that his young brother looked like becoming a Coll Punt. The immemorial league between us was strained, all but broken.

All this was cruelly complicated by the fact that relations between my father and my brother were never before or since so bad as at this time; and Wyvern was behind that too. My brother's reports had grown worse and worse; and the tutor to whom he had now been sent confirmed them to the extent of saying that he seemed to have learned almost nothing at school. Nor was that all. Sentences savagely underlined in my father's copy of *The Lanchester Tradition* reveal his thoughts. They are passages about a certain glazed insolence, an elaborate, heartless flippancy, which the reforming Headmaster in that story encountered in the Bloods of the school he wished to reform. That was how my father envisaged my brother at this period: flippant, languid, emptied of the intellectual interests which had appeared in his earlier boyhood, immovable, indifferent to all real values, and urgent in his demand for a motor-bicycle.

It was, of course, to turn us into public school boys that my father had originally sent us to Wyvern; the finished product appalled him. It is a familiar tragi-comedy and you can study it in Lockhart; Scott laboured hard to make his son a hussar, but when the actual hussar was presented to him, Scott sometimes forgot the illusion of being an aristocrat and became once more a respectable Edinburgh lawyer with strong views about Puppyism. So in our family. Mispronunciation was one of my father's favourite rhetorical weapons. He now always sounded the first syllable of Wyvern wrongly. I can still hear him growl, 'Wyvernian affectation.' In proportion as my brother's tone became languid and urbanely weary, so my father's voice became more richly and energetically Irish, and all manner of strange music from his boyhood in Cork and Dublin forced its way up through the more recent Belfastian crust.

During these miserable debates I occupied a most unfortunate position. To have been on my father's side and against my brother I should have had to unmake myself; it was a state of parties outside my whole philosophy of domestic politics. It was all very disagreeable.

Yet out of this 'unpleasantness' (a favourite word of my father's) there sprang what I still reckon, by merely natural standards, the most fortunate thing that ever happened to me. The tutor (in Surrey) to whom my brother had been sent was one of my father's oldest friends. He had been headmaster of Lurgan when my father was a boy there. In a surprisingly short time he so re-built and extended the ruins of my brother's education that he not only passed into Sandhurst but was placed among those very few candidates at the top of the list who received prize cadetships. I do not think my father ever did justice to my brother's achievement; it came at a time when the gulf between them was too wide, and when they were friends again it had become ancient history. But he saw very clearly what it proved about the exceptional powers of his teacher. At the same time, he was almost as sick as I of the very name of Wyvern. And I never ceased, by letter and by word of mouth, to beg that I might be taken away. All these factors urged him to the decision which he now made. Might it not after all be best to give me my desire? To have done with school for good and send me also to Surrey to read for the University with Mr Kirkpatrick? He did not form this plan without much doubt and hesitation. He did his best to put all the risks before me: the dangers of solitude, the sudden change from the life and bustle of a great school (which change I might not like so much as I anticipated), the possibly deadening effect of living with only an old man and his old wife for company. Should I really be happy with no companions of my own age? I tried to look very grave at these questions.

But it was all imposture. My heart laughed. Happy without other boys? Happy without toothache, without chilblains, happy without pebbles in my shoes? And so the arrangement was made. If it had had nothing else to recommend it, the mere thought, 'Never, never, never, shall I have to play games again,' was enough to transport me. If you want to know how I felt, imagine your own feelings on waking one morning to find that income tax or unrequited love had somehow vanished from the world.

I should be sorry if I were understood to think, or if I encouraged any reader in thinking, that this invincible dislike of doing things with a bat or a ball were other than a misfortune. Not, indeed, that I allow to games any of the moral and almost mystical virtues which schoolmasters claim for them; they seem to me to lead to ambition, jealousy, and embittered partisan feeling, quite as often as to anything else. Yet not to like them is a misfortune, because it cuts you off from companionship with many excellent people who can be approached in no other way. A misfortune, not a vice; for it is involuntary. I had tried to like games and failed. That impulse had been left out of my make-up; I was to games, as the proverb has it, like an ass to the harp.

It is a curious truth, noticed by many writers, that good fortune is nearly always followed by more good fortune, and bad, by more bad. About the same time that my father decided to send me to Mr Kirkpatrick, another great good came to me. Many chapters ago I mentioned a boy who lived near us and who had tried, quite unsuccessfully, to make friends with my brother and myself. His name was Arthur and he was my brother's exact contemporary; he and I had been at Campbell together though we never met. I think it was shortly before the beginning of my last term at Wyvern that I received a message saying that Arthur was in bed, convalescent, and would welcome a visit. I can't remember what led me to accept this invitation, but for some reason I did.

I found Arthur sitting up in bed. On the table beside him lay a copy of *Myths of the Norsemen*.

'Do *you* like that?' said I.

'Do *you* like that?' said he.

Next moment the book was in our hands, our heads were bent close together, we were pointing, quoting, talking—soon almost shouting—discovering in a torrent of questions that we liked not only the same thing, but the same parts of it and in the same way; that both knew the stab of Joy and that, for both, the arrow was shot from the North. Many thousands of people have had the experience of finding the first friend, and it is none the less a wonder; as great a wonder (*pace* the novelists) as first love, or even a greater. I had been so far from thinking such a friend possible that I had never even longed for one; no more than I longed to be King of England. If I had found that Arthur had independently built up an exact replica of the Boxonian world I should not really have been much more surprised. Nothing, I suspect, is more astonishing in any man's life than the discovery that there do exist people very, very like himself.

During my last few weeks at Wyvern strange stories began to appear in the papers, for this was the summer of 1914. I remember how a friend and I puzzled over a column that bore the headline 'Can England keep out of it?' 'Keep out of it?' said he, 'I don't see how she can get into it.' Memory paints the last hours of that term in slightly apocalyptic colours, and perhaps memory lies. Or perhaps for me it was apocalyptic enough to know that I was leaving, to see all those hated things for the last time; yet not simply (at that moment) to hate them. There is a 'rumness', a ghostliness, about even a Windsor chair when it says, 'You will not see me again.' Early in the holidays we declared war. My brother, then on leave from Sandhurst, was recalled. Some weeks later I went to Mr Kirkpatrick at Great Bookham in Surrey.

IX

THE GREAT KNOCK

You will often meet with characters in nature so
extravagant that a discreet poet would not venture
to set them upon the stage.

LORD CHESTERFIELD

On a September day, having crossed to Liverpool and
reached London, I made my way to Waterloo and ran
down to Great Bookham. I had been told that Surrey was
'suburban', and the landscape that actually flitted past the
windows astonished me. I saw steep little hills, watered
valleys, and wooded commons which ranked by my
Wyvernian and Irish standards as forests; bracken everywhere; a world of red and russet and yellowish greens.
Even the sprinkling of suburban villas (much rarer then
than now) delighted me. These timbered and red-tiled
houses, embosomed in trees, were wholly unlike the stuc-
coed monstrosities which formed the suburbs of Belfast.
Where I had expected gravel drives and iron gates and

interminable laurels and monkey puzzlers, I saw crooked paths running up or down hill from wicket gates, between fruit trees and birches. By a severer taste than mine these houses would all be mocked perhaps; yet I cannot help thinking that those who designed them and their gardens achieved their object, which was to suggest Happiness. They filled me with a desire for that domesticity which, in its full development, I had never known; they set one thinking of tea trays.

At Bookham I was met by my new teacher—'Kirk' or 'Knock' or the Great Knock as my father, my brother, and I all called him. We had heard about him all our lives and I therefore had a very clear impression of what I was in for. I came prepared to endure a perpetual luke-warm shower bath of sentimentality. That was the price I was ready to pay for the infinite blessedness of escaping school; but a heavy price. One story of my father's, in particular, gave me the most embarrassing forebodings. He had loved to tell how once at Lurgan, when he was in some kind of trouble or difficulty, the Old Knock, or the dear Old Knock, had drawn him aside and there 'quietly and naturally' slid his arm round him and rubbed his dear old whiskers against my father's youthful cheek and whispered a few words of comfort . . . And here was Bookham at last, and there was the arch-sentimentalist himself waiting to meet me.

He was over six feet tall, very shabbily dressed (like a gardener, I thought), lean as a rake, and immensely muscular. His wrinkled face seemed to consist entirely of muscles, so far as it was visible; for he wore moustache and side whiskers with a clean-shaven chin like the Emperor Franz Joseph. The whiskers, you will understand, concerned me very much at that moment. My cheek already tingled in anticipation. Would he begin at once? There would be tears for certain; perhaps worse things. It is one of my life-long weaknesses that I never could endure the embrace or kiss of my own sex. (An unmanly weakness, by the way; Aeneas, Beowulf, Roland, Launcelot, Johnson, and Nelson knew nothing of it.)

Apparently, however, the old man was holding his fire. We shook hands, and though his grip was like iron pincers it was not lingering. A few minutes later we were walking away from the station.

'You are now,' said Kirk, 'proceeding along the principal artery between Great and Little Bookham.'

I stole a glance at him. Was this geographical exordium a heavy joke? Or was he trying to conceal his emotions? His face, however, showed only an inflexible gravity. I began to 'make conversation' in the deplorable manner which I had acquired at those evening parties and indeed found increasingly necessary to use with my father. I said

I was surprised at the 'scenery' of Surrey; it was much 'wilder' than I had expected.

'Stop!' shouted Kirk with a suddenness that made me jump. 'What do you mean by wildness and what grounds had you for not expecting it?'

I replied I don't know what, still 'making conversation'. As answer after answer was torn to shreds it at last dawned upon me that he really wanted to know. He was not making conversation, not joking, not snubbing me; he wanted to know. I was stung into attempting a real answer. A few passes sufficed to show that I had no clear and distinct idea corresponding to the word 'wildness', and that, in so far as I had any idea at all, 'wildness' was a singularly inept word. 'Do you not see, then,' concluded the Great Knock, 'that your remark was meaningless?' I prepared to sulk a little, assuming that the subject would now be dropped. Never was I more mistaken in my life. Having analysed my terms, Kirk was proceeding to deal with my proposition as a whole. On what had I based (but he pronounced it *baized*) my expectations about the Flora and Geology of Surrey? Was it maps, or photographs, or books? I could produce none. It had, heaven help me, never occurred to me that what I called my thoughts needed to be 'baized' on anything. Kirk once more drew a conclusion—without the slightest sign of emotion, but equally without the slightest concession to what I thought good manners: 'Do you not see, then, that you had no right to have any opinion whatever on the subject?'

By this time our acquaintance had lasted about three and a half minutes; but the tone set by this first conversation was preserved without a single break during all the years I spent at Bookham. Anything more grotesquely unlike the 'dear Old Knock' of my father's reminiscences could not be conceived. Knowing my father's invariable intention of veracity and also knowing what strange transformations every truth underwent when once it entered his mind, I am sure he did not mean to deceive us. But if Kirk at any time of his life took a boy aside and there 'quietly and naturally' rubbed the boy's face with his whiskers, I shall as easily believe that he sometimes varied the treatment by quietly and naturally standing on his venerable and egg-bald head.

If ever a man came near to being a purely logical entity, that man was Kirk. Born a little later, he would have been a Logical Positivist. The idea that human beings should exercise their vocal organs for any purpose except that of communicating or discovering truth was to him preposterous. The most casual remark was taken as a summons to disputation. I soon came to know the differing values of his three openings. The loud cry of 'Stop!' was flung in to arrest a torrent of verbiage which could not be endured a moment longer; not because it fretted his patience (he never thought of that) but because it was wasting time, darkening counsel. The hastier and quieter 'Excuse!' (i.e., 'Excuse me') ushered in a correction or distinction merely parenthetical and betokened that, thus set right, your remark might still, without absurdity, be allowed to reach completion. The most encouraging of all was, 'I hear you.' This meant that your remark was significant and only required refutation; it had risen to the dignity of error. Refutation (when we got so far) always followed the same lines. Had I read this? Had I studied that? Had I any statistical evidence? Had I any evidence in my own experience? And so to the almost inevitable conclusion, 'Do you not see then that you had no right, etc.'

Some boys would not have liked it; to me it was red beef and strong beer. I had taken it for granted that my leisure hours at Bookham would be passed in 'grown-up conversation'. And that, as you know already, I had no taste for. In my experience it meant conversation about politics, money, deaths, and digestion. I assumed that a taste for it, as for eating mustard or reading newspapers, would develop in me when I grew older (so far, all three expectations have been disappointed). The only two kinds of talk I wanted were the almost purely imaginative and the almost purely rational; such talk as I had about Boxen with my brother or about Valhalla with Arthur, on the one hand, or such talk as I had had with my uncle Gussie about astronomy on the other. I could never have gone far in any science because on the path of every science the lion Mathematics lies in wait for you. Even in Mathematics, whatever could be done by mere reasoning (as in simple geometry) I did with delight; but the moment calculation came in I was helpless. I grasped the principles but my answers were always wrong. Yet though I could never have been a scientist, I had scientific as well as imaginative impulses, and I loved ratiocination. Kirk excited and satisfied one side of me. Here was talk that was really about something. Here was a man who thought not about you but about what you said. No doubt I snorted and bridled a little at some of my tossings; but, taking it all in all, I loved the treatment. After being knocked down sufficiently often I began to know a few guards and blows, and to put on intellectual muscle. In the end, unless I flatter myself, I became a not contemptible sparring partner. It was a great day when the man who had so long been engaged in exposing my vagueness at last cautioned me against the dangers of excessive subtlety.

If Kirk's ruthless dialectic had been merely a pedagogic instrument I might have resented it. But he knew no other way of talking. No age or sex was spared the elenchus. It was a continuous astonishment to him that anyone should not desire to be clarified or corrected. When a very dignified neighbour, in the course of a Sunday call, observed with an air of finality, 'Well, well, Mr Kirkpatrick, it takes all sorts to make a world. You are a Liberal and I am a Conservative; we naturally look at the facts from different angles,' Kirk replied, 'What do you mean? Are you asking me to picture Liberals and Conservatives playing peep-ho at a rectangular Fact from opposite sides of a table?' If an unwary visitor, hoping to waive a subject, observed, 'Of course, I know opinions differ—' Kirk would raise both hands and exclaim, 'Good heavens! I have no *opinions* on any subject whatsoever.' A favourite maxim was, 'You can have enlightenment for ninepence but you prefer ignorance.' The commonest metaphors would be questioned till some bitter truth had been forced from its hiding place. 'These fiendish German atrocities—' 'But are not fiends a figment of the imagination?'—'Very well, then; these brutal atrocities—' 'But none of the brutes does anything of the kind!'—'Well, what am I to call them?' 'Is it not plain that we must call them simply *Human*?' What excited his supreme contempt was the conversation of other Headmasters, which he had sometimes had to endure at conferences when he himself was Head of

Lurgan. 'They would come and ask me, 'What attitude do you adopt to a boy who does so-and-so?' Good Heavens! As if I ever adopted an attitude to anybody or anything!' Sometimes, but rarely, he was driven to irony. On such occasions his voice became even weightier than usual and only the distention of his nostrils betrayed the secret to those who knew him. It was in such fashion that he produced his *dictum*, 'The Master of Balliol is one of the most important beings in the universe.'

It will be imagined that Mrs Kirkpatrick led a somewhat uneasy life: witness the occasion on which her husband by some strange error found himself in the drawing-room at the beginning of what his lady had intended to be a bridge party. About half an hour later she was observed to leave the room with a remarkable expression on her face; and many hours later still the Great Knock was discovered sitting on a stool in the midst of seven elderly ladies ('ful drery was hire chere') begging them to clarify their terms.

I have said that he was almost wholly logical; but not quite. He had been a Presbyterian and was now an Atheist. He spent Sunday, as he spent most of his time on weekdays, working in his garden. But one curious trait from his Presbyterian youth survived. He always, on Sundays, gardened in a different, and slightly more respectable, suit.

An Ulster Scot may come to disbelieve in God, but not to wear his week-day clothes on the Sabbath.

Having said that he was an Atheist, I hasten to add that he was a 'Rationalist' of the old, high and dry nineteenth-century type. For Atheism has come down in the world since those days, and mixed itself with politics and learned to dabble in dirt. The anonymous donor who now sends me anti-God magazines hopes, no doubt, to hurt the Christian in me; he really hurts the ex-Atheist. I am ashamed that my old mates and (which matters much more) Kirk's old mates should have sunk to what they are now. It was different then; even McCabe wrote like a man. At the time when I knew him, the fuel of Kirk's Atheism was chiefly of the anthropological and pessimistic kind. He was great on *The Golden Bough* and Schopenhauer.

The reader will remember that my own Atheism and Pessimism were fully formed before I went to Bookham. What I got there was merely fresh ammunition for the defence of a position already chosen. Even this I got indirectly from the tone of his mind or independently from reading his books. He never attacked religion in my presence. It is the sort of fact that no one would infer from an outside knowledge of my life, but it is a fact.

I arrived at Gastons (so the Knock's house was called) on a Saturday, and he announced that we would begin

Homer on Monday. I explained that I had never read a word in any dialect but the Attic, assuming that when he knew this he would approach Homer through some preliminary lessons on the Epic language. He replied merely with a sound very frequent in his conversation which I can only spell 'Huh'. I found this rather disquieting; and I woke on Monday saying to myself, 'Now for Homer. Golly!' The name struck awe into my soul. At nine o'clock we sat down to work in the little upstairs study which soon became so familiar to me. It contained a sofa (on which we sat side by side when he was working with me), a table and chair (which I used when I was alone), a bookcase, a gas stove, and a framed photograph of Mr Gladstone. We opened our books at *Iliad*, Book I. Without a word of introduction Knock read aloud the first twenty lines or so in the 'new' pronunciation, which I had never heard before. Like Smewgy, he was a chanter; less mellow in voice, yet his full gutturals and rolling R's and more varied vowels seemed to suit the bronze-age epic as well as Smewgy's honey tongue had suited Horace. For Kirk, even after years of residence in England, spoke the purest Ulster. He then translated, with a few, a very few explanations, about a hundred lines. I had never seen a classical author taken in such large gulps before. When he had finished he handed me over Crusius' *Lexicon* and, having told me to go through again as much as I could of what he had done, left the room. It seems an odd method of teaching, but it worked. At first I could travel only a very short way along the trail he had blazed, but every day I could travel further. Presently I could travel the whole way. Then I could go a line or two beyond his furthest North. Then it became a kind of game to see how far beyond. He appeared at this stage to value speed more than absolute accuracy. The great gain was that I very soon became able to understand a great deal without (even mentally) translating it; I was beginning to think in Greek. That is the great Rubicon to cross in learning any language. Those in whom the Greek word lives only while they are hunting for it in the lexicon, and who then substitute the English word for it, are not reading the Greek at all; they are only solving a puzzle. The very formula, 'Naus means a ship', is wrong. Naus and ship both mean a thing, they do not mean one another. Behind Naus, as behind navis or naca, we want to have a picture of a dark, slender mass with sail or oars, climbing the ridges, with no officious English word intruding.

We now settled into a routine which has ever since served in my mind as an archetype, so that what I still mean when I speak of a 'normal' day (and lament that normal days are so rare) is a day of the Bookham pattern.

For if I could please myself I would always live as I lived there. I would choose always to breakfast at exactly eight and to be at my desk by nine, there to read or write till one. If a cup of good tea or coffee could be brought me about eleven, so much the better. A step or so out of doors for a pint of beer would not do quite so well; for a man does not want to drink alone and if you meet a friend in the tap-room the break is likely to be extended beyond its ten minutes. At one precisely lunch should be on the table; and by two at the latest I would be on the road. Not, except at rare intervals, with a friend. Walking and talking are two very great pleasures, but it is a mistake to combine them. Our own noise blots out the sounds and silences of the outdoor world; and talking leads almost inevitably to smoking, and then farewell to nature as far as one of our senses is concerned. The only friend to walk with is one (such as I found, during the holidays, in Arthur) who so exactly shares your taste for each mood of the country-side that a glance, a halt, or at most a nudge, is enough to assure us that the pleasure is shared. The return from the walk, and the arrival of tea, should be exactly coincident, and not later than a quarter past four. Tea should be taken in solitude, as I took it at Bookham on those (happily numerous) occasions when Mrs Kirkpatrick was out; the Knock himself disdained this meal. For eating and reading are two pleasures that combine admirably. Of course not all books are suitable for mealtime reading. It would be a kind of blasphemy to read poetry at table. What one wants is a gossipy, formless book which can be opened anywhere. The ones I learned so to use at Bookham were Boswell, and a translation of Herodotus, and Lang's *History of English Literature. Tristram Shandy, Elia,* and the *Anatomy of Melancholy* are all good for the same purpose. At five a man should be at work again, and at it till seven. Then, at the evening meal and after, comes the time for talk, or, failing that, for lighter reading; and unless you are making a night of it with your cronies (and at Bookham I had none) there is no reason why you should ever be in bed later than eleven. But when is a man to write his letters? You forget that I am describing the happy life I led with Kirk or the ideal life I would live now if I could. And it is an essential of the happy life that a man would have almost no mail and never dread the postman's knock. In those blessed days I received, and answered, only two letters a week; one from my father, which was a matter of duty, and one from Arthur, which was the high light of the week, for we poured out to each other on paper all the delight that was intoxicating us both. Letters from my brother, now on active service, were longer and rarer, and so were my replies.

Such is my ideal, and such then (almost) was the reality, of 'settled, calm, Epicurean life'. It is no doubt for my own good that I have been so generally prevented from leading it, for it is a life almost entirely selfish. Selfish, not self-centred: for in such a life my mind would be directed towards a thousand things, not one of which is myself. The distinction is not unimportant. One of the happiest men and most pleasing companions I have ever known was intensely selfish. On the other hand I have known people capable of real sacrifice whose lives were nevertheless a misery to themselves and to others, because self-concern and self-pity filled all their thoughts. Either condition will destroy the soul in the end. But till the end, give me the man who takes the best of everything (even at my expense) and then talks of other things, rather than the man who serves me and talks of himself, and whose very kindnesses are a continual reproach, a continual demand for pity, gratitude, and admiration.

Kirk did not, of course, make me read nothing but Homer. The Two Great Bores (Demosthenes and Cicero) could not be avoided. There were (oh glory!) Lucretius, Catullus, Tacitus, Herodotus. There was Virgil, for whom I still had no true taste. There were Greek and Latin compositions. (It is a strange thing that I have contrived to reach my late fifties without ever reading one word of Caesar.)

There were Euripides, Sophocles, Aeschylus. In the evenings there was French with Mrs Kirkpatrick, treated
much as her husband treated Homer. We got through a
great many good novels in this way and I was soon buying French books on my own. I had hoped there would be
English essays, but whether because he felt he could not
endure mine or because he soon guessed that I was already
only too proficient in that art (which he almost certainly
despised) Kirk never set me one. For the first week or
so he gave me directions about my English reading, but
when he discovered that, left to myself, I was not likely
to waste my time, he gave me absolute freedom. Later
in my career we branched out into German and Italian.
Here his methods were the same. After the very briefest
contact with Grammars and Exercises I was plunged into
Faust and the *Inferno*. In Italian we succeeded. In German
I have little doubt that we should equally have succeeded
if I had stayed with him a little longer. But I left too soon
and my German has remained all my life that of a schoolboy. Whenever I have set about rectifying this, some other
and more urgent task has always interrupted me.

But Homer came first. Day after day and month after
month we drove gloriously onward, tearing the whole
Achilleid out of the *Iliad* and tossing the rest on one side,
and then reading the *Odyssey* entire, till the music of the

thing and the clear, bitter brightness that lives in almost every formula had become part of me. Of course my appreciation was very romanticised—the appreciation of a boy soaked in William Morris. But this slight error saved me from that far deeper error of 'classicism' with which the Humanists have hoodwinked half the world. I cannot therefore deeply regret the days when I called Circe a 'wise-wife' and every marriage a 'high-tide'. That has all burned itself out and left no snuff, and I can now enjoy the *Odyssey* in a maturer way. The wanderings mean as much as ever they did; the great moment of 'eucatastrophe' (as Professor Tolkien would call it) when Odysseus strips off his rags and bends the bow, means more; and perhaps what now pleases me best of all is those exquisite Charlotte M. Yonge families at Pylos and elsewhere. How rightly Sir Maurice Powicke says, 'There have been civilised people in all ages.' And let us add, 'In all ages they have been surrounded by barbarism.'

Meanwhile, on afternoons and on Sundays, Surrey lay open to me. County Down in the holidays and Surrey in the term—it was an excellent contrast. Perhaps, since their beauties were such that even a fool could not force them into competition, this cured me once and for all of the pernicious tendency to compare and to prefer—an operation that does little good even when we are dealing

with works of art and endless harm when we are dealing with nature. Total surrender is the first step towards
the fruition of either. Shut your mouth; open your eyes
and ears. Take in what is there and give no thought to
what might have been there or what is somewhere else.
That can come later, if it must come at all. (And notice
here how the true training for anything whatever that is
good always prefigures and, if submitted to, will always
help us in, the true training for the Christian life. That is
a school where they can always use your previous work
whatever subject it was on.) What delighted me in Surrey
was its intricacy. My Irish walks commanded large hori-
zons and the general lie of land and sea could be taken
in at a glance: I will try to speak of them later. But in
Surrey the contours were so tortuous, the little valleys
so narrow, there was so much timber, so many villages
concealed in woods or hollows, so many field paths, sunk
lanes, dingles, copses, such an unpredictable variety of
cottage, farmhouse, villa, and country seat, that the whole
thing could never lie clearly in my mind, and to walk in it
daily gave one the same sort of pleasure that there is in the
labyrinthine complexity of Malory or the *Faerie Queene*.
Even where the prospect was tolerably open, as when I
sat looking down on the Leatherhead and Dorking valley
from Polesden Lacey, it always lacked the classic compre-

hensibility of the Wyvern landscape. The valley twisted away southward into another valley, a train thudded past invisible in a wooded cutting, the opposite ridge concealed its bays and promontories. This, even on a summer morning. But I remember more dearly autumn afternoons in bottoms that lay intensely silent under old and great trees, and especially the moment, near Friday Street, when our party (that time I was not alone) suddenly discovered, from recognising a curiously shaped stump, that we had travelled round in a circle for the last half-hour; or one frosty sunset over the Hog's Back at Guildford. On a Saturday afternoon in winter, when nose and fingers might be pinched enough to give an added relish to the anticipation of tea and fireside, and the whole week-end's reading lay ahead, I suppose I reached as much happiness as is ever to be reached on earth. And especially if there were some new, long-coveted book awaiting me.

For I had forgotten. When I spoke of the post I forgot to tell you that it brought parcels as well as letters. Every man of my age has had in his youth one blessing for which our juniors may well envy him: we grew up in a world of cheap and abundant books. Your *Everyman* was then a bare shilling, and, what is more, always in stock; your *World's Classic, Muses' Library, Home University Library, Temple Classic*, Nelson's French series, Bohn, and

Longman's Pocket Library, at proportionate prices. All the money I could spare went in postal orders to Messrs Denny of the Strand. No days, even at Bookham, were happier than those on which the afternoon post brought me a neat little parcel in dark grey paper. Milton, Spenser, Malory, *The High History of the Holy Grail*, the *Laxdale Saga*, Ronsard, Chénier, Voltaire, *Beowulf* and *Gawain and the Green Knight* (both in translations), Apuleius, the *Kalevala*, Herrick, Walton, Sir John Mandeville, Sidney's *Arcadia*, and nearly all of Morris, came volume by volume into my hands. Some of my purchases proved disappointments and some went beyond my hopes, but the undoing of the parcel always remained a delicious moment. On my rare visits to London, I looked at Messrs Denny in the Strand with a kind of awe; so much pleasure had come from it.

Smewgy and Kirk were my two greatest teachers. Roughly, one might say (in medieval language) that Smewgy taught me Grammar and Rhetoric and Kirk taught me Dialectic. Each had, and gave me, what the other lacked. Kirk had none of Smewgy's graciousness or delicacy, and Smewgy had less humour than Kirk. It was a saturnine humour. Indeed he was very like Saturn—not the dispossessed King of Italian legend, but grim old Cronos, Father Time himself with scythe and hourglass.

The bitterest, and also funniest, things came out when he had risen abruptly from table (always before the rest of us) and stood ferreting in a villainous old tobacco jar on the mantelpiece for the dottles of former pipes which it was his frugal habit to use again. My debt to him is very great, my reverence to this day undiminished.

X

FORTUNE'S SMILE

The fields, the floods, the heavens, with one consent
Did seeme to laugh on me, and favour mine intent.

                                                    SPENSER

At the same time that I exchanged Wyvern for Bookham I
also exchanged my brother for Arthur as my chief companion. My brother, as you know, was serving in France.
From 1914 to 1916, which is the Bookham period, he
becomes a figure that at rare intervals appears unpredicted
on leave, in all the glory of a young officer, with what then
seemed unlimited wealth at his command, and whisks me
off to Ireland. Luxuries hitherto unknown to me, such as
first-class railway carriages and sleeping cars, glorify these
journeys. You will understand that I had been crossing the
Irish Sea six times a year since I was nine. My brother's
leaves now often added journeys extraordinary. That is
why my memory is stored with ship's-side images to a
degree unusual for such an untravelled man. I have only to

close my eyes to see if I choose, and sometimes whether I choose or no, the phosphorescence of a ship's wash, the mast unmoving against the stars though the water is rushing past us, the long salmon-coloured rifts of dawn or sunset on the horizon of cold grey-green water, or the astonishing behaviour of land as you approach it, the promontories that walk out to meet you, the complex movements and final disappearance of the mountains further inland.

These leaves were of course a great delight. The strains that had been developing (thanks to Wyvern) before my brother went to France were forgotten. There was a tacit determination on both sides to revive, for the short time allowed us, the classic period of our boyhood. As my brother was in the RASC, which in those days was reckoned a safe place to be, we did not feel that degree of anxiety about him which most families were suffering at this time. There may have been more anxiety in the unconscious than came out in fully waking thought. That, at least, would explain an experience I had, certainly once, and perhaps more often; not a belief, nor quite a dream, but an impression, a mental image, a haunting, which on a bitter winter night at Bookham represented my brother hanging about the garden and calling—or rather trying to call, but as in Virgil's Hell *inceptus clamor frustratur hiantem,* a bat's cry is all that comes. There hung over this image an atmosphere which I dislike as much as any I ever breathed, a blend of the macabre and the weakly, wretchedly, hopelessly pathetic—the dreary miasma of the Pagan Hades.

Though my friendship with Arthur began from an identity of taste on a particular point, we were sufficiently different to help one another. His home-life was almost the opposite of mine. His parents were members of the Plymouth Brothers, and he was the youngest of a large family; his home, nevertheless, was almost as silent as ours was noisy. He was at this time working in the business of one of his brothers, but his health was delicate and after an illness or two he was withdrawn from it. He was a man of more than one talent: a pianist and, in hope, a composer, and also a painter. One of our earliest schemes was that he should make an operatic score for *Loki Bound*—a project which, of course, after an extremely short and happy life, died a painless death. In literature he influenced me more, or more permanently, than I did him. His great defect was that he cared very little for verse. Something I did to mend this, but less than I wished. He, on the other hand, side by side with his love for myth and marvel, which I fully shared, had another taste which I lacked till I met him and with which, to my great good, he infected me for life.

This was the taste for what he called 'the good, solid, old books', the classic English novelists. It is astonishing how I had avoided them before I met Arthur. I had been persuaded by my father to read *The Newcomes* when I was rather too young for it and never tried Thackeray again till I was at Oxford. He is still antipathetic to me, not because he preaches but because he preaches badly. Dickens I looked upon with a feeling of horror, engendered by long poring over the illustrations before I had learned to read. I still think them depraved. Here, as in Walt Disney, it is not the ugliness of the ugly figures but the simpering dolls intended for our sympathy which really betray the secret (not that Walt Disney is not far superior to the illustrators of Dickens). Of Scott I knew only a few of the medieval, that is, the weakest, novels. Under Arthur's influence I read at this time all the best Waverleys, all the Brontës, and all the Jane Austens. They provided an admirable complement to my more fantastic reading, and each was the more enjoyed for its contrast to the other. The very qualities which had previously deterred me from such books Arthur taught me to see as their charm. What I would have called their 'stodginess' or 'ordinariness' he called 'Homeliness'—a key word in his imagination. He did not mean merely Domesticity, though that came into it. He meant the rooted quality which attaches them to all our simple experiences, to weather, food, the family, the neighbourhood. He could get endless enjoyment out of the opening sentence *of Jane Eyre,* or that other opening sentence in one of Hans Andersen's stories, 'How it did rain, to be sure.' The mere word 'beck' in the Brontës was a feast to him; and so were the schoolroom and kitchen scenes. This love of the 'Homely' was not confined to literature; he looked for it in out-of-door scenes as well and taught me to do the same.

Hitherto my feelings for nature had been too narrowly romantic. I had attended almost entirely to what I thought awe-inspiring, or wild, or eerie, and above all to distance. Hence mountains and clouds were my especial delight; the sky was, and still is, to me one of the principal elements in any landscape, and long before I had seen them all named and sorted out in *Modern Painters* I was very attentive to the different qualities, and different heights, of the cirrus, the cumulus, and the rain-cloud. As for the Earth, the country I grew up in had everything to encourage a romantic bent, had indeed done so ever since I first looked at the unattainable Green Hills through the nursery window. For the reader who knows those parts it will be enough to say that my main haunt was the Holywood Hills—the irregular polygon you would have described if you drew a line from Stormont to Comber, from Comber to Newtownards, from Newtownards to Scrabo, from Scrabo to Craigantlet, from Craigantlet to Holywood, and thence through Knocknagonney back to Stormont. How to suggest it all to a foreigner I hardly know.

First of all, it is by southern English standards bleak. The woods, for we have a few, are of small trees, rowan and birch and small fir. The fields are small, divided by ditches with ragged sea-nipped hedges on top of them. There is a good deal of gorse and many outcroppings of rock. Small abandoned quarries, filled with cold-looking water, are surprisingly numerous. There is nearly always a wind whistling through the grass. Where you see a man ploughing there will be gulls following him and pecking at the furrow. There are no field-paths or rights of way, but that does not matter for everyone knows you—or if they do not know you, they know your kind and understand that you will shut gates and not walk over crops. Mushrooms are still felt to be common property, like the air. The soil has none of the rich chocolate or ochre you find in parts of England: it is pale—what Dyson calls 'the ancient, bitter earth'. But the grass is soft, rich, and sweet, and the cottages, always white-washed and single storeyed and roofed with blue slate, light up the whole landscape.

Although these hills are not very high, the expanse seen from them is huge and various. Stand at the northeastern extremity where the slopes go steeply down to Holywood. Beneath you is the whole expanse of the Lough. The Antrim coast twists sharply to the north and out of sight; green, and humble in comparison, Down curves away southward. Between the two the Lough merges into the sea, and if you look carefully on a good day you can even see Scotland, phantom-like on the horizon. Now come further to the south and west. Take your stand at the isolated cottage which is visible from my father's house and overlooks our whole suburb, and which everyone calls The Shepherd's Hut, though we are not really a shepherd country. You are still looking down on the Lough, but its mouth and the sea are now hidden by the shoulder you have just come from, and it might (for all you see) be a landlocked lake. And here we come to one of those great contrasts which have bitten deeply into my mind—Niflheim and Asgard, Britain and Logres, Handramit and Harandra, air and ether, the low world and the high. Your horizon from here is the Antrim Mountains, probably a uniform mass of greyish blue, though if it is a sunny day you may just trace on the Cave Hill the distinction between the green slopes that climb two-thirds of the way to the summit and the cliff wall that perpendicularly accomplishes the rest. That is one beauty; and here where you stand is another, quite different and even more dearly loved—sunlight and grass and dew, crowing cocks and gaggling ducks. In between them, on the flat floor of the Valley at your feet, a forest of factory chimneys, gantries, and giant cranes rising out of a welter of mist, lies Belfast. Noises come up from it continually, whining and screeching of trams, clatter of horse traffic on uneven sets, and, dominating all else, the continual throb and stammer of the great shipyards. And because we have heard this all our lives it does not, for us, violate the peace of the hill-top; rather, it emphasises it, enriches the contrast, sharpens the dualism. Down in that 'smoke and stir' is the hated office to which Arthur, less fortunate than I, must return to-morrow; for it is only one of his rare holidays that allows us to stand here together on a week-day morning. And down there too are the barefoot old women, the drunken men stumbling in and out of the 'spirit grocers' (Ireland's horrible substitute for the kindly English 'pub'), the straining, overdriven horses, the hard-faced rich women—all the world which Alberich created when he cursed love and twisted the gold into a ring.

Now step a little way—only two fields and across a lane and up to the top of the bank on the far side—and you will see, looking south with a little east in it, a different world. And having seen it, blame me if you can for being a romantic. For here is the thing itself, utterly irresistible,

the way to the world's end, the land of longing, the breaking and blessing of hearts. You are looking across what
may be called, in a certain sense, the plain of Down, and
seeing beyond it the Mourne Mountains.

It was K.—that is, Cousin Quartus' second daughter,
the Valkyrie—who first expounded to me what this plain
of Down is really like. Here is the recipe for imagining it.
Take a number of medium-sized potatoes and lay them
down (one layer of them only) in a flat-bottomed tin
basin. Now shake loose earth over them till the potatoes
themselves, but not the shape of them, is hidden; and of
course the crevices between them will now be depressions
of earth. Now magnify the whole thing till those crevices
are large enough to conceal each its stream and its hud-
dle of trees. And then, for colouring, change your brown
earth into the chequered pattern of fields, always small
fields (a couple of acres each), with all their normal variety
of crop, grass, and plough. You have now got a picture of
the 'plain' of Down, which is a plain only in this sense that
if you were a very large giant you would regard it as level
but very ill to walk on—like cobbles. And now remember that every cottage is white. The whole expanse laughs
with these little white dots; it is like nothing so much as
the assembly of white foam-caps when a fresh breeze is
on a summer sea. And the roads are white too; there is no

tarmac yet. And because the whole country is a turbulent democracy of little hills, these roads shoot in every direction, disappearing and reappearing. But you must not spread over this landscape your hard English sunlight; make it paler, make it softer, blur the edges of the white cumuli, cover it with watery gleams, deepening it, making all unsubstantial. And beyond all this, so remote that they seem fantastically abrupt at the very limit of your vision, imagine the mountains. They are no stragglers. They are steep and compact and pointed and toothed and jagged. They seem to have nothing to do with the little hills and cottages that divide you from them. And sometimes they are blue, sometimes violet; but quite often they look transparent—as if huge sheets of gauze had been cut into mountainous shapes and hung up there, so that you could see through them the light of the invisible sea at their backs.

I number it among my blessings that my father had no car, while yet most of my friends had, and sometimes took me for a drive. This meant that all these distant objects could be visited just enough to clothe them with memories and not impossible desires, while yet they remained ordinarily as inaccessible as the Moon. The deadly power of rushing about wherever I pleased had not been given me. I measured distances by the standard of man, man walking

on his two feet, not by the standard of the internal com-
bustion engine. I had not been allowed to deflower the
very idea of distance; in return I possessed 'infinite riches'
in what would have been to motorists 'a little room'. The
truest and most horrible claim made for modern transport is that it 'annihilates space'. It does. It annihilates
one of the most glorious gifts we have been given. It is a
vile inflation which lowers the value of distance, so that a
modern boy travels a hundred miles with less sense of liberation and pilgrimage and adventure than his grandfather
got from travelling ten. Of course if a man hates space and
wants it to be annihilated, that is another matter. Why not
creep into his coffin at once? There is little enough space
there.

Such were my outdoor delights before I met Arthur,
and all these he shared and confirmed. And in his search
for the Homely he taught me to see other things as well.
But for him I should never have known the beauty of the
ordinary vegetables that we destine to the pot. 'Drills,' he
used to say. 'Just ordinary drills of cabbages—what can
be better?' And he was right. Often he recalled my eyes
from the horizon just to look through a hole in a hedge,
to see nothing more than a farmyard in its mid-morning
solitude, and perhaps a grey cat squeezing its way under
a barn door, or a bent old woman with a wrinkled, moth-

erly face coming back with an empty bucket from the pig-sty. But best of all we liked it when the Homely and the unhomely met in sharp juxtaposition; if a little kitchen garden ran steeply up a narrowing *enclave* of fertile ground surrounded by outcroppings and furze, or some shivering quarry pool under a moonrise could be seen on our left, and on our right the smoking chimney and lamplit window of a cottage that was just settling down for the night.

Meanwhile, on the continent, the unskilled butchery of the first German War went on. As it did so and as I began to foresee that it would probably last till I reached military age, I was compelled to make a decision which the law had taken out of the hands of English boys of my own age; for in Ireland we had no conscription. I did not much plume myself even then for deciding to serve, but I did feel that the decision absolved me from taking any further notice of the war. For Arthur, whose heart hopelessly disqualified him, there was no such question. Accordingly I put the war on one side to a degree which some people will think shameful and some incredible. Others will call it a flight from reality. I maintain that it was rather a treaty with reality, the fixing of a frontier. I said to my country, in effect, 'You shall have me on a certain date, not before. I will die in your wars if need be, but till then I shall live my own life. You may have my body, but not my mind.

I will take part in battles but not read about them.' If this attitude needs excusing I must say that a boy who is unhappy at school inevitably learns the habit of keeping the future in its place; if once he began to allow infiltrations from the coming term into the present holidays he would despair. Also, the Hamilton in me was always on guard against the Lewis; I had seen enough of the self-torturing temperament.

No doubt, even if the attitude was right, the quality in me which made it so easy to adopt is somewhat repellent. Yet, even so, I can hardly regret having escaped the appalling waste of time and spirit which would have been involved in reading the war news or taking more than an artificial and formal part in conversations about the war. To read without military knowledge or good maps accounts of fighting which were distorted before they reached the Divisional general and further distorted before they left him and then 'written up' out of all recognition by journalists, to strive to master what will be contradicted the next day, to fear and hope intensely on shaky evidence, is surely an ill use of the mind. Even in peace-time I think those are very wrong who say that schoolboys should be encouraged to read the newspapers. Nearly all that a boy reads there in his teens will be known before he is twenty to have been false in emphasis and interpretation, if not in fact as well, and most of it will have lost all importance. Most of what he remembers he will therefore have to unlearn; and he will probably have acquired an incurable taste for vulgarity and sensationalism and the fatal habit of fluttering from paragraph to paragraph to learn how an actress has been divorced in California, a train derailed in France, and quadruplets born in New Zealand.

I was now happier than I had ever been. All the sting had been drawn from the beginning of term. Yet the homecoming at its end remained almost as joyful as before. The holidays grew better and better. Our grown-up friends, and especially my cousins at Mountbracken, now seemed less grown up—for one's immediate elders grow downwards or backwards to meet one at that age. There were many merry meetings, much good talk. I discovered that other people besides Arthur loved books that I loved. The horrible old 'social functions', the dances, were at an end, for my father now allowed me to refuse the invitations. All my engagements were now pleasant ones, within a small circle of people who were all inter-married, or very old neighbours, or (the women any-way) old schoolfellows. I am shy of mentioning them. Of Mountbracken I have had to speak because the story of my life could not be told without it; beyond that I hesitate to go. Praise of one's friends is near impertinence. I cannot tell you here of Janie M. nor of her mother, nor of Bill and Mrs Bill. In novels, provincial-suburban society is usually painted grey to black. I have not found it so. I think we Strandtown and Belmont people had among us as much kindness, wit, beauty, and taste as any circle of the same size that I have ever known.

At home the real separation and apparent cordiality between my father and myself continued. Every holidays I came back from Kirk with my thoughts and my speech a little clearer, and this made it progressively less possible to have any real conversation with my father. I was far too young and raw to appreciate the other side of the account, to weigh the rich (if vague) fertility, the generosity and humour of my father's mind against the dryness, the rather deathlike lucidity, of Kirk's. With the cruelty of youth I allowed myself to be irritated by traits in my father which, in other elderly men, I have since regarded as lovable foibles. There were so many unbridgeable misunderstandings. Once I received a letter from my brother in my father's presence which he immediately demanded to see. He objected to some expressions in it about a third person. In defence of them I pleaded that they had not been addressed to him. 'What nonsense!' answered my father. 'He knew you would show me the letter, and intended you to show me the letter.' In reality, as I well knew, my brother had foolishly gambled on the chance that it would arrive when my father was out. But this my father could not conceive. He was not overriding by authority a claim to privacy which he disallowed; he could not imagine any-one making such a claim.

My relations to my father help to explain (I am not suggesting that they excuse) one of the worst acts of my life. I allowed myself to be prepared for confirmation, and confirmed, and to make my first Communion, in total disbelief, acting a part, eating and drinking my own con-demnation. As Johnson points out, where courage is not, no other virtue can survive except by accident. Cowardice drove me into hypocrisy and hypocrisy into blasphemy. It is true that I did not and could not then know the real nature of the thing I was doing: but I knew very well that I was acting a lie with the greatest possible solemnity. It seemed to me impossible to tell my father my real views. Not that he would have stormed and thundered like the traditional orthodox parent. On the contrary, he would (at first) have responded with the greatest kindness. 'Let's talk the whole thing over,' he would have said. But it would have been quite impossible to drive into his head my real position. The thread would have been lost almost at once, and the answer implicit in all the quotations, anecdotes, and reminiscences which would have poured

over me would have been one I then valued not a straw—
the beauty of the Authorised Version, the beauty of the
Christian tradition and sentiment and character. And later,
when this failed, when I still tried to make my exact points
clear, there would have been anger between us, thunder
from him and a thin, peevish rattle from me. Nor could
the subject, once raised, ever have been dropped again. All
this, of course, ought to have been dared rather than the
thing I did. But at the time it seemed to me impossible.
The Syrian captain was forgiven for bowing in the house
of Rimmon. I am one of many who have bowed in the
house of the real God when I believed Him to be no more
than Rimmon.

During the week-ends and evenings I was closely teth-
ered to my father and felt this something of a hardship,
since these were the times when Arthur was most often
accessible. My week-days continued to supply me with
a full ration of solitude. I had, to be sure, the society of
Tim, who ought to have been mentioned far sooner. Tim
was our dog. He may hold a record for longevity among
Irish terriers since he was already with us when I was at
Oldie's and did not die till 1922. But Tim's society did not
amount to much. It had long since been agreed between
him and me that he should not be expected to accompany
me on walks. I went a good deal further than he liked, for

his shape was already that of a bolster, or even a barrel, on four legs. Also, I went to places where other dogs might be met; and though Tim was no coward (I have seen him fight like a demon on his home ground) he hated dogs. In his walking days he had been known, on seeing a dog far ahead, to disappear behind the hedge and re-emerge a hundred yards later. His mind had been formed during our schooldays and he had perhaps learned his attitude to other dogs from our attitude to other boys. By now he and I were less like master and dog than like two friendly visitors in the same hotel. We met constantly, passed the time of day, and parted with much esteem to follow our own paths. I think he had one friend of his own species, a neighbouring red setter; a very respectable, middle-aged dog. Perhaps a good influence; for poor Tim, though I loved him, was the most undisciplined, unaccomplished, and dissipated-looking creature that ever went on four legs. He never exactly obeyed you; he sometimes agreed with you.

The long hours in the empty house passed delightfully in reading and writing. I was in the midst of the Romantics now. There was a humility in me (as a reader) at that time which I shall never recapture. Some poems I could not enjoy as well as others. It never occurred to me that these might be the inferior ones; I merely thought that I was getting tired of my author or was not in the right mood. The *longueurs* of Endymion I attributed wholly to myself. The 'swoony' element in Keats' sensuality (as when Porphyro grows 'faint') I tried hard to like, and failed. I thought — though I have forgotten why — that Shelley must be better than Keats and was sorry I liked him less. But my great author at this period was William Morris. I had met him first in quotation in books on Norse Mythology; that led me to *Sigurd the Volsung*. I did not really like this as much as I tried to, and I think I now know why: the metre does not satisfy my ear. But then, in Arthur's bookcase, I found *The Well at the World's End*. I looked — I read chapter headings — I dipped — and next day I was off into town to buy a copy of my own. Like so many new steps it appeared to be partly a revival — 'Knights in Armour' returning from a very early period of my childhood. After that I read all the Morris I could get, *Jason, The Earthly Paradise,* the prose romances. The growth of the new delight is marked by my sudden realisation, almost with a sense of disloyalty, that the letters WILLIAM MORRIS were coming to have at least as potent a magic in them as WAGNER.

One other thing that Arthur taught me was to love the bodies of books. I had always respected them. My brother and I might cut up step-ladders without scruple; to have thumb-marked or dog's-eared a book would have filled us with shame. But Arthur did not merely respect, he was enamoured; and soon, I too. The set up of the page, the feel and smell of the paper, the differing sounds that different papers make as you turn the leaves, became sensuous delights. This revealed to me a flaw in Kirk. How often have I shuddered when he took a new classical text of mine in his gardener's hands, bent back the boards till they creaked, and left his sign on every page.

'Yes, I remember,' said my father. 'That was Old Knock's one fault.'

'A bad one,' said I.

'An all but unforgivable one,' said my father.

XI

CHECK

When bale is at highest, boote is at next.

SIR ALDINGAR

The history of Joy, since it came riding back to me on huge waves of Wagnerian music and Norse and Celtic mythology several chapters ago, must now be brought up to date.

I have already hinted how my first delight in Valhalla and Valkyries began to turn itself imperceptibly into a scholar's interest in them. I got about as far as a boy who knew no old Germanic language could get. I could have faced a pretty stiff examination in my subject. I would have laughed at popular bunglers who confused the late mythological Sagas with the classic Sagas, or the Prose with the Verse Edda, or even, more scandalously, Edda with Saga. I knew my way about the Eddaic cosmos, could locate each of the roots of the Ash, and knew who ran up and down it. And only very gradually did I realise that all this was something quite different from the original Joy.

And I went on adding detail to detail, progressing towards the moment when 'I should know most and should least enjoy'. Finally I woke from building the temple to find that the God had flown. Of course I did not put it that way. I would have said simply that I didn't get the old thrill. I was in the Wordsworthian predicament, lamenting that 'a glory' had passed away.

Thence arose the fatal determination to recover the old thrill, and at last the moment when I was compelled to realise that all such efforts were failures. I had no lure to which the bird would come. And now, notice my blindness. At that very moment there arose the memory of a place and time at which I had tasted the lost Joy with unusual fullness. It had been a particular hill-walk on a morning of white mist. The other volumes of the *Ring* (*The Rheingold* and *The Valkyrie*) had just arrived as a Christmas present from my father, and the thought of all the reading before me, mixed with the coldness and loneliness of the hillside, the drops of moisture on every branch, and the distant murmur of the concealed town, had produced a longing (yet it was also fruition) which had flowed over from the mind and seemed to involve the whole body. That walk I now remembered. It seemed to me that I had tasted heaven then. If only such a moment could return! But what I never realised was that it had returned—that the remembering of that walk was itself a new experience of just the same kind. True, it was desire, not possession. But then what I had felt on the walk had also been desire, and only possession in so far as that kind of desire is itself desirable, is the fullest possession we can know on earth; or rather, because the very nature of Joy makes nonsense of our common distinction between having and wanting. There, to have is to want and to want is to have. Thus, the very moment when I longed to be so stabbed again, was itself again such a stabbing. The Desirable which had once alighted on Valhalla was now alighting on a particular moment of my own past; and I would not recognise him there because, being an idolater and a formalist, I insisted that he ought to appear in the temple I had built him; not knowing that he cares only for temples building and not at all for temples built. Wordsworth, I believe, made this mistake all his life. I am sure that all that sense of the loss of vanished vision which fills *The Prelude* was itself vision of the same kind, if only he could have believed it.

In my scheme of thought it is not blasphemous to compare the error which I was making with that error which the angel at the Sepulchre rebuked when he said to the women, 'Why seek ye the living among the dead? He is not here, He is risen.' The comparison is of course between something of infinite moment and something very small;

like comparison between the Sun and the Sun's reflection in a dewdrop. Indeed, in my view, very like it, for I do not think the resemblance between the Christian and the merely imaginative experience is accidental. I think that all things, in their way, reflect heavenly truth, the imagination not least. *Reflect* is the important word. This lower life of the imagination is not[1] a beginning of, nor a step towards, the higher life of the spirit, merely an image. In me, at any rate, it contained no element either of belief or of ethics; however far pursued, it would never have made me either wiser or better. But it still had, at however many removes, the shape of the reality it reflected.

If nothing else suggests this resemblance it is at least suggested by the fact that we can make exactly the same mistakes on both levels. You will remember how, as a schoolboy, I had destroyed my religious life by a vicious subjectivism which made 'realisations' the aim of prayer; turning away from God to seek states of mind, and trying to produce those states of mind by 'maistry'. With unbelievable folly I now proceeded to make exactly the same blunder in my imaginative life; or rather the same pair of blunders. The first was made at the very moment when I

---

[1] i.e., not necessarily and by its own nature. God can cause it to be such a beginning.

formulated the complaint that the 'old thrill' was becoming rarer and rarer. For by that complaint I smuggled in the assumption that what I wanted was a 'thrill', a state of my own mind. And there lies the deadly error. Only when your whole attention and desire are fixed on something else—whether a distant mountain, or the past, or the gods of Asgard—does the 'thrill' arise. It is a by-product. Its very existence presupposes that you desire not it but something other and outer. If by any perverse askesis or the use of any drug it could be produced from within, it would at once be seen to be of no value. For take away the object, and what, after all, would be left?—a whirl of images, a fluttering sensation in the diaphragm, a momentary abstraction. And who could want that? This, I say, is the first and deadly error, which appears on every level of life and is equally deadly on all, turning religion into a self-caressing luxury and love into auto-eroticism. And the second error is, having thus falsely made a state of mind your aim, to attempt to produce it. From the fading of the Northernness I ought to have drawn the conclusion that the Object, the Desirable, was further away, more external, less subjective, than even such a comparatively public and external thing as a system of mythology—had, in fact, only shone through that system. Instead, I concluded that it was a mood or state within myself which might turn

up in any context. To 'get it again' became my constant
endeavour; while reading every poem, hearing every piece
of music, going for every walk, I stood anxious sentinel at
my own mind to watch whether the blessed moment was
beginning and to endeavour to retain it if it did. Because I
was still young and the whole world of beauty was opening before me, my own officious obstructions were often
swept aside and, startled into self-forgetfulness, I again
tasted Joy. But far more often I frightened it away by my
greedy impatience to snare it, and, even when it came,
instantly destroyed it by introspection, and at all times
vulgarised it by my false assumption about its nature.

One thing, however, I learned, which has since saved
me from many popular confusions of mind. I came to
know by experience that it is not a disguise of sexual
desire. Those who think that if adolescents were all provided with suitable mistresses we should soon hear no
more of 'immortal longings' are certainly wrong. I learned
this mistake to be a mistake by the simple, if discreditable,
process of repeatedly making it. From the Northernness
one could not easily have slid into erotic fantasies without noticing the difference; but when the world of Morris
became the frequent medium of Joy, this transition became
possible. It was quite easy to think that one desired those
forests for the sake of their female inhabitants, the garden

of Hesperus for the sake of his daughters, Hylas' river for the river nymphs. I repeatedly followed that path — to the end. And at the end one found pleasure; which immediately resulted in the discovery that pleasure (whether that pleasure or any other) was not what you had been looking for. No moral question was involved; I was at this time as nearly non-moral on that subject as a human creature can be. The frustration did not consist in finding a 'lower' pleasure instead of a 'higher'. It was the irrelevance of the conclusion that marred it. The hounds had changed scent. One had caught the wrong quarry. You might as well offer a mutton chop to a man who is dying of thirst as offer sexual pleasure to the desire I am speaking of. I did not recoil from the erotic conclusion with chaste horror, exclaiming, 'Not that!' My feelings could rather have been expressed in the words, 'Quite. I see. But haven't we wandered from the real point?' Joy is not a substitute for sex; sex is very often a substitute for Joy. I sometimes wonder whether all pleasures are not substitutes for Joy.

Such, then, was the state of my imaginative life; over against it stood the life of my intellect. The two hemispheres of my mind were in the sharpest contrast. On the one side a many-islanded sea of poetry and myth; on the other a glib and shallow 'rationalism'. Nearly all that I loved I believed to be imaginary; nearly all that I believed to be real I thought grim and meaningless. The exceptions were certain people (whom I loved and believed to be real) and nature herself. That is, nature as she appeared to the senses. I chewed endlessly on the problem: 'How can it be so beautiful and also so cruel, wasteful and futile?' Hence at this time I could almost have said with Santayana, 'All that is good is imaginary; all that is real is evil.' In one sense nothing less like a 'flight from reality' could be conceived. I was so far from wishful thinking that I hardly thought anything true unless it contradicted my wishes.

Hardly, but not quite. For there was one way in which the world, as Kirk's rationalism taught me to see it, gratified my wishes. It might be grim and deadly but at least it was free from the Christian God. Some people (not all) will find it hard to understand why this seemed to me such an overwhelming advantage. But you must take into account both my history and my temperament. The period of faith which I had lived through at Oldie's had contained a good deal of fear. And by now, looking back on that fear, and egged on by Shaw and Voltaire and Lucretius with his *Tantum religio*, I greatly exaggerated that element in my memory and forgot the many other elements which had been combined with it. At all costs I was anxious that those full-moonlit nights in the dormitory should never come again. I was also, as you may remember, one whose negative demands were more violent than his positive, far more eager to escape pain than to achieve happiness, and feeling it something of an outrage that I had been created without my own permission. To such a craven the materialist's universe had the enormous attraction that it offered you limited liabilities. No strictly infinite disaster could overtake you in it. Death ended all. And if ever finite disasters proved greater than one wished to bear, suicide would always be possible. The horror of the Christian universe was that it had no door marked *Exit*. It was also perhaps not unimportant that the externals of Christianity made no appeal to my sense of beauty. Oriental imagery and style largely repelled me; and for the rest, Christianity was mainly associated for me with ugly architecture, ugly music, and bad poetry. Wyvern Priory and Milton's verse were almost the only points at which Christianity and beauty had overlapped in my experience. But, of course, what mattered most of all was my deep-seated hatred of authority, my monstrous individualism, my lawlessness. No word in my vocabulary expressed deeper hatred than the word *Interference*. But Christianity placed at the centre what then seemed to me a transcendental Interferer. If its picture were true then no sort of 'treaty with reality' could ever be possible. There was no region even in the innermost depth of one's soul (nay, there least of all) which one could surround with a barbed wire fence and guard with a notice No Admittance. And that was what I wanted; some area, however small, of which I could say to all other beings, 'This is my business and mine only.'

In this respect, and this only at first, I may have been guilty of wishful thinking. Almost certainly I was. The materialist conception would not have seemed so immensely probable to me if it had not favoured at least one of my wishes. But the difficulty of explaining even a boy's thought entirely in terms of his wishes is that on such large questions as these he always has wishes on both sides. Any conception of reality which a sane mind can admit must favour some of its wishes and frustrate others. The materialistic universe had one great, negative attraction to offer me. It had no other. And this had to be accepted; one had to look out on a meaningless dance of atoms (remember, I was reading Lucretius), to realise that all the apparent beauty was a subjective phosphorescence, and to relegate everything one valued to the world of mirage. That price I tried loyally to pay. For I had learned something from Kirk about the honour of the intellect and the shame of voluntary inconsistency. And, of course, I exulted with youthful and vulgar pride in what I thought my enlightenment. In argument with Arthur I was a very swashbuckler. Most of it, as I now see, was incredibly crude and silly. I was in that state of mind in which a boy thinks it extremely telling to call God *jahveh* and Jesus *Yeshua*.

Looking back on my life now, I am astonished that I did not progress into the opposite orthodoxy—did not become a Leftist, Atheist, satiric Intellectual of the type we all know so well. All the conditions seem to be present. I had hated my public school. I hated whatever I knew or imagined of the British Empire. And though I took very little notice of Morris' socialism (there were too many things in him that interested me far more) continual reading of Shaw had brought it about that such embryonic political opinions as I had were vaguely socialistic. Ruskin had helped me in the same direction. My lifelong fear of sentimentalism ought to have qualified me to become a vigorous 'debunker'. It is true that I hated the Collective as much as any man can hate anything; but I certainly did not then realise its relations to socialism. I suppose that my Romanticism was destined to divide me from the orthodox Intellectuals as soon as I met them; and also that a mind so little sanguine as mine about the future and about common action could only with great difficulty be made revolutionary.

Such, then, was my position: to care for almost nothing but the gods and heroes, the garden of the Hesperides, Launcelot and the Grail, and to believe in nothing but atoms and evolution and military service. At times the strain was severe, but I think this was a wholesome severity. Nor do I believe that the intermittent wavering in my materialistic 'faith' (so to call it) which set in towards the end of the Bookham period would ever have arisen simply from my wishes. It came from another source.

Among all the poets whom I was reading at this time (I read *The Faerie Queene* and *The Earthly Paradise* entire) there was one who stood apart from the rest. Yeats was this poet. I had been reading him for a long time before I discovered the difference, and perhaps I should never have discovered it if I had not read his prose as well: things like *Rosa Alchemica* and *Per Amica Silentia Lunae.* The difference was that Yeats believed. His 'ever living ones' were not merely feigned or merely desired. He really thought that there was a world of beings more or less like them, and that contact between that world and ours was possible. To put it quite plainly, he believed seriously in Magic. His later career as a poet has somewhat obscured that phase in popular estimates of him, but there is no doubt about the fact—as I learned when I met him some years later. Here was a pretty kettle of fish. You will understand that my rationalism was inevitably based on what I believed to be the findings of the sciences, and those findings, not being a scientist, I had to take on trust—in fact, on authority. Well, here was an opposite authority. If he had been a Christian I should have discounted his testimony, for I thought I had the Christians 'placed' and disposed of for ever. But I now learned that there were people, not traditionally orthodox, who nevertheless rejected the whole Materialist philosophy out of hand. And I was still very ingenuous. I had no conception of the amount of nonsense written and printed in the world. I regarded Yeats as a learned, responsible writer: what he said must be worthy of consideration. And after Yeats I plunged into Maeterlinck; quite innocently and naturally since everyone was reading him at that time and since I made a point of including a fair amount of French in my diet. In Maeterlinck I came up against Spiritualism, Theosophy, and Pantheism. Here once more was a responsible adult (and not a Christian) who believed in a world behind, or around, the material world. I must do myself the justice of saying that I did not give my assent categorically. But a drop of disturbing doubt fell into my Materialism. It was merely a 'Perhaps'. Perhaps (oh joy!) there was, after all, 'something else'; and (oh reassurance!) perhaps it had nothing to do with Christian Theology. And as soon as I paused on that 'Perhaps', inevitably all the old Occultist lore, and all the old excitement which the Matron at Chartres had innocently aroused in me, rose out of the past.

Now the fat was in the fire with a vengeance. Two things hitherto widely separated in my mind rushed together: the imaginative longing for Joy, or rather the longing which *was* Joy, and the ravenous, quasi-prurient desire for the Occult, the Preternatural as such. And with these there came (less welcome) some stirring of unease, some of the immemorial fear we have all known in the nursery, and (if we are honest) long after the nursery age. There is a kind of gravitation in the mind whereby good rushes to good and evil to evil. This mingled repulsion and desire drew towards them everything else in me that was bad. The idea that if there were Occult knowledge it was known to very few and scorned by the many became an added attraction; 'we few', you will remember, was an evocative expression for me. That the means should be Magic—the most exquisitely unorthodox thing in the world, unorthodox both by Christian and by Rationalist standards—of course appealed to the rebel in me. I was already acquainted with the more depraved side of Romanticism; had read *Anactoria,* and Wilde, and pored upon Beardsley, not hitherto attracted, but making no moral judgement. Now I thought I began to see the point of it. In a word, you have already had in this story the World and the Flesh; now came the Devil. If there had been in the neighbourhood some elder person who dabbled in dirt of the Magical kind (such have a good nose for potential disciples) I might now be a Satanist or a maniac.

In actual fact I was wonderfully protected; and this spiritual debauch had in the end one rather good result. I was protected, first by ignorance and incapacity. Whether Magic were possible or not, I at any rate had no teacher to start me on the path. I was protected also by cowardice; the reawakened terrors of childhood might add a spice to my greed and curiosity as long as it was daylight. Alone, and in darkness, I used my best endeavours to become a strict Materialist again; not always with success. A 'Perhaps' is quite enough for the nerves to work upon. But my best protection was the known nature of Joy. This ravenous desire to break the bounds, to tear the curtain, to be in the secret revealed itself, more and more clearly the longer I indulged it, to be quite different from the longing that is Joy. Its coarse strength betrayed it. Slowly, and with many relapses, I came to see that the magical conclusion was just as irrelevant to Joy as the erotic conclusion had been. Once again one had changed scents. If circles and pentangles and the Tetragrammaton had been tried and had in fact raised, or seemed to raise, a spirit, that might have been—if a man's nerves could stand it—extremely interesting; but the real Desirable would have evaded one, the real Desire would have been left saying, 'What is this to me?'

What I like about experience is that it is such an honest thing. You may take any number of wrong turnings; but keep your eyes open and you will not be allowed to go very far before the warning signs appear. You may have deceived yourself, but experience is not trying to deceive you. The universe rings true wherever you fairly test it.

The other results of my glance into the dark room were as follows. First, I now had both a fresh motive for wishing Materialism to be true and a decreased confidence that it was. The fresh motive came, as you have divined, from those fears which I had so wantonly stirred up from their sleeping place in the memories of childhood; behaving like a true Lewis who will not leave well alone. Every man who is afraid of spooks will have a reason for wishing to be a Materialist; that creed promises to exclude the bogies. As for my shaken confidence, it remained in the form of a 'Perhaps', stripped of its directly and grossly magical 'affect'—a pleasing possibility that the Universe might combine the snugness of Materialism here and now with . . . well, with I didn't know what; somewhere or something beyond, 'the unimaginable lodge for solitary thinkings'. this was very bad. I was beginning to try to have it both ways: to get the comforts both of a materialist and of a spiritual philosophy without the rigours of either. But the second result was better. I had learned a wholesome antipathy to everything occult and magical which was to stand me in good stead when, at Oxford, I came to meet Magicians, Spiritualists, and the like. Not that the ravenous lust was never to tempt me again but that I now knew it for a temptation. And above all, I now knew that Joy did not point in that direction.

You might sum up the gains of this whole period by saying that henceforward the Flesh and the Devil, though they could still tempt, could no longer offer me the supreme bribe. I had learned that it was not in their gift. And the World had never even pretended to have it.

And then, on top of this, in superabundance of mercy, came that event which I have already more than once attempted to describe in other books. I was in the habit of walking over to Leatherhead about once a week and sometimes taking the train back. In summer I did so chiefly because Leatherhead boasted a tiny swimming bath; better than nothing to me who had learned to swim almost before I can remember and who, till middle age and rheumatism crept upon me, was passionately fond of being in water. But I went in winter, too, to look for books and to get my hair cut. The evening that I now speak of was in October. I and one porter had the long, timbered platform of Leatherhead station to ourselves. It was getting just dark enough for the smoke of an engine to glow red on the underside with the reflection of the furnace. The hills beyond the Dorking Valley were of a blue so intense as to be nearly violet and the sky was green with frost. My ears tingled with the cold. The glorious week-end of reading was before me. Turning to the bookstall, I picked out an Everyman in a dirty jacket, *Phantastes, a Faerie Romance*, George MacDonald. Then the train came in. I can still remember the voice of the porter calling out the village names, Saxon and sweet as a nut—'Bookham, Effingham, Horsley train.' That evening I began to read my new book.

The woodland journeyings in that story, the ghostly enemies, the ladies both good and evil, were close enough to my habitual imagery to lure me on without the perceptions of a change. It is as if I were carried sleeping across the frontier, or as if I had died in the old country and could never remember how I came alive in the new. For in one sense the new country was exactly like the old. I met there all that had already charmed me in Malory, Spenser, Morris, and Yeats. But in another sense all was changed. I did not yet know (and I was long in learning) the name of the new quality, the bright shadow, that rested on the travels of Anodos. I do now. It was Holiness. For the first time the song of the sirens sounded like the voice of my mother or my nurse. Here were old wives' tales; there was nothing to be proud of in enjoying them. It was as though the voice which had called to me from the world's end were now speaking at my side. It was with me in the room, or in my own body, or behind me. If it had once eluded me by its distance, it now eluded me by proximity—something too near to see, too plain to be understood, on this side of knowledge. It seemed to have been always with me; if I could ever have turned my head quick enough I should have seized it. Now for the first time I felt that it was out of reach not because of something I could not do but because of something I could not stop doing. If I could only leave off, let go, unmake myself, it would be there. Meanwhile, in this new region all the confusions that had hitherto perplexed my search for Joy were disarmed. There was no temptation to confuse the scenes of the tale with the light that rested upon them, or to suppose that they were put forward as realities, or even to dream that if they had been realities and I could reach the woods where Anodos journeyed I should thereby come a step nearer to my desire. Yet, at the same time, never had the wind of Joy blowing through any story been less separable from the story itself. Where the god and the *idolon* were most nearly one there was least danger of confounding them. Thus, when the great moments came I did not break away from the woods and cottages that I read of to seek some bodiless light shining beyond them, but gradually, with a swelling continuity (like the sun at mid-morning burning through a fog) I found the light shining on those woods and cottages, and then on my own past life, and on the quiet room where I sat and on my old teacher where he nodded above his little *Tacitus*. For I now perceived that while the air of the new region made all my erotic and magical perversions of Joy look like sordid trumpery, it had no such disenchanting power over the bread upon the table or the coals in the grate. That was the marvel. Up till now each visitation of Joy had left the common world momentarily a desert— 'The first touch of the earth went nigh to kill.' Even when real clouds or trees had been the material of the vision, they had been so only by reminding me of another world; and I did not like the return to ours. But now I saw the bright shadow coming out of the book into the real world and resting there, transforming all common things and yet itself unchanged. Or, more accurately, I saw the common things drawn into the bright shadow. *Unde hoc mihi?* In the depth of my disgraces, in the then invincible ignorance of my intellect, all this was given me without asking, even without consent. That night my imagination was, in a certain sense, baptised; the rest of me, not unnaturally, took longer. I had not the faintest notion what I had let myself in for by buying *Phantastes*.

XII

GUNS AND GOOD COMPANY

La compagnie, de tant d'hommes vous plaist, nobles,
jeunes, actifs; la liberté de cette conversation sans
art, et une façon de vie masle et sans cérémonie.

MONTAIGNE

The old pattern began to repeat itself. The Bookham days, like a longer and more glorious holidays, drew to their end; a scholarship examination and, after that, the Army, loomed behind them like a grimmer term. The good time had never been better than in its last months. I remember, in particular, glorious hours of bathing in Donegal. It was surf bathing: not the formal affair with boards that you have now, but mere rough and tumble, in which the waves, the monstrous, emerald, deafening waves, are always the winner, and it is at once a joke, a terror, and a joy to look over your shoulder and see (too late) one breaker of such sublime proportions that you would have avoided him had you known he was coming. But they gather themselves up, preeminent above their fellows, as suddenly and unpredictably as a revolution.

It was late in the winter term of 1916 that I went to Oxford to sit for my scholarship examination. Boys who have faced this ordeal in peace-time will not easily imagine the indifference with which I went. This does not mean that I underestimated the importance (in one sense) of succeeding. I knew very well by now that there was hardly any position in the world save that of a don in which I was fitted to earn a living, and that I was staking everything on a game in which few won and hundreds lost. As Kirk had said of me in a letter to my father (I did not, of course, see it till many years later), 'You may make a writer or a scholar of him, but you'll not make anything else. You may make up your mind to *that.*' And I knew this myself; sometimes it terrified me. What blunted the edge of it now was that whether I won a scholarship or no I should next year go into the army; and even a temper more sanguine than mine could feel in 1916 that an infantry subaltern would be insane to waste anxiety on anything so hypothetical as his post-war life. I once tried to explain this to my father; it was one of the attempts I often made (though doubtless less often than I ought) to break through the artificiality of our intercourse and admit him to my real life. It was a total failure. He replied at once with fatherly counsels about the necessity of hard work and concentration, the amount that he had already spent in educating me, the very moderate, nay, negligible, assistance he would be able to give me in later life. Poor man! He misjudged me sadly if he thought that idleness at my book was among my many vices. And how, I asked myself, could he expect the winning or losing of a scholarship to lose none of its importance when life and death were the real issues? The truth is, I think, that while death (mine, his, everyone's) was often vividly present to him as a subject of anxiety and other emotions, it had no place in his mind as a sober, matter-of-fact contingency from which consequences could be drawn. At any rate the conversation was a failure. It shipwrecked on the old rock. His intense desire for my total confidence co-existed with an inability to listen (in any strict sense) to what I said. He could never empty, or silence, his own mind to make room for an alien thought.

My first taste of Oxford was comical enough. I had made no arrangements about quarters and, having no more luggage than I could carry in my hand, I sallied out of the railway station on foot to find either a lodginghouse or a cheap hotel; all agog for 'dreaming spires' and 'last enchantments'. My first disappointment at what I saw could be dealt with. Towns always show their worst face to the railway. But as I walked on and on I became more bewildered. Could this succession of mean shops really be Oxford? But I still went on, always expecting the next turn to reveal the beauties, and reflecting that it was a much larger town than I had been led to suppose. Only when it became obvious that there was very little town left ahead of me, that I was in fact getting to open country, did I turn round and look. There, behind me, far away, never more beautiful since, was the fabled cluster of spires and towers. I had come out of the station on the wrong side and been all this time walking into what was even then the mean and sprawling suburb of Botley. I did not see to what extent this little adventure was an allegory of my whole life. I merely walked back to the station, some-what footsore, took a hansom, and asked to be driven to 'some place where I can get rooms for a week, please'. The method, which I should now think hazardous, was a complete success, and I was soon at tea in comfortable lodgings. The house is still there, the first on the right as you turn into Mansfield Road out of Holywell. I shared the sitting-room with another candidate, a man from Cardiff College, which he pronounced to be architecturally superior to anything in Oxford. His learning terrified me, but he was an agreeable man. I have never seen him since.

It was very cold and next day snow began to fall, turning pinnacles into wedding-cake decorations. The examination was held in the Hall of Oriel, and we all wrote in greatcoats and mufflers and wearing at least our left-hand gloves. The Provost, old Phelps, gave out the papers. I remember very little about them, but I suppose I was outshone in pure classics by many of my rivals and succeeded on my general knowledge and dialectics. I had the impression that I was doing badly. Long years (or years that seemed long) with the Knock had cured me of my defensive Wyvernian priggery, and I no longer supposed other boys to be ignorant of what I knew. Thus the essay was on a quotation from Johnson. I had read several times the Boswellian conversation in which it occurred and was able to replace the whole question in that context; but I never thought that this (any more than a fairish knowledge of Schopenhauer) would gain me any particular credit. It was a blessed state to be in, but for the moment depressing. As I left the Hall after that essay I heard one candidate say to his friend, 'I worked in all my stuff about Rousseau and the Social Contract.' That struck dismay into my soul, for though I had dabbled (not to my good) in the *Confessions* I knew nothing of the *Contrat Social.* At the beginning of the morning a nice Harrovian had whispered to me, 'I don't even know if it's Sam or Ben.'

In my innocence I explained to him that it was Sam and could not be Ben because Ben was spelled without an H. I did not think there could be any harm in giving away such information.

When I arrived home I told my father that I had almost certainly failed. It was an admission calculated to bring out all his tenderness and chivalry. The man who could not understand a boy's taking his own possible, or probable, death into account could very well understand a child's disappointment. Not a word was now heard of expenses and difficulties; nothing but consolation, reassurance, and affection. Then, almost on Christmas Eve, we heard that 'Univ.' (University College) had elected me.

Though I was now a scholar of my College I still had to pass 'Responsions', which involved elementary mathematics. To prepare for this I returned after Christmas for one last term with Kirk—a golden term, poignantly happy under the approaching shadow. At Easter I was handsomely ploughed in Responsions, having been unable as usual to get my sums right. 'Be more careful', was the advice that everyone gave me, but I found it useless. The more care I took the more mistakes I made; just as, to this day, the more anxiously I fair copy a piece of writing the more certain I am to make a ghastly clerical error in the very first line.

In spite of this I came into residence in the summer (Trinity) term of 1917; for the real object now was simply to enter the University Officers' Training Corps as my most promising route into the Army. My first studies at Oxford, nevertheless, still had Responsions in view. I read algebra (devil take it!) with old Mr Campbell of Hertford who turned out to be a friend of our dear friend Janie M. That I never passed Responsions is certain, but I cannot remember whether I again sat for it and was again ploughed. The question became unimportant after the war, for a benevolent decree exempted ex-Service men from taking it. Otherwise, no doubt, I should have had to abandon the idea of going to Oxford.

I was less than a term at Univ. when my papers came through and I enlisted; and the conditions made it a most abnormal term. Half the College had been converted into a hospital and was in the hands of the RAMC. In the remaining portion lived a tiny community of undergraduates—two of us not yet of military age, two unfit, one a Sinn-Feiner who would not fight for England, and a few other oddments which I never quite placed. We dined in the little lecture room which is now a passage between Common Room and Hall. Small though our numbers were (about eight) we were rather distinguished, for we included E. V. Gordon, afterwards Professor of

English at Manchester, and A. C. Ewing, the Cambridge philosopher; also that witty and kindly man, Theobald Butler, skilled in turning the most lurid limericks into Greek verse. I enjoyed myself greatly; but it bore little resemblance to normal undergraduate life and was for me an unsettled, excited, and generally useless period. Then came the Army. By a remarkable turn of fate this did not mean removal from Oxford. I was drafted into a Cadet Battalion whose billet was Keble.

I passed through the ordinary course of training (a mild affair in those days compared with that of the recent war) and was commissioned as a Second Lieutenant in the Somerset Light Infantry, the old XIIIth Foot. I arrived in the front line trenches on my nineteenth birthday (November 1917), saw most of my service in the villages before Arras—Fampoux and Monchy—and was wounded at Mt Bernenchon, near Lillers, in April 1918.

I am surprised that I did not dislike the Army more. It was, of course, detestable. But the words 'of course' drew the sting. That is where it differed from Wyvern. One did not expect to like it. Nobody said you ought to like it. Nobody pretended to like it. Everyone you met took it for granted that the whole thing was an odious necessity, a ghastly interruption of rational life. And that made all the difference. Straight tribulation is easier to bear than tribulation which advertises itself as pleasure. The one breeds *camaraderie* and even (when intense) a kind of love between the fellow-sufferers; the other, mutual distrust, cynicism, concealed and fretting resentment. And secondly, I found my military elders and betters incomparably nicer than the Wyvern Bloods. This is no doubt because Thirty is naturally kinder to Nineteen than Nineteen is to Thirteen: it is really grown-up and does not need to reassure itself. But I am inclined to think that my face had altered. That 'look' which I had so often been told to 'take off it' had apparently taken itself off—perhaps when I read *Phantastes.* There is even some evidence that it had been succeeded by a look which excited either pity or kindly amusement. Thus, on my very first night in France, in a vast marquee or drill hall where about a hundred officers were to sleep on plank beds, two middle-aged Canadians at once took charge of me and treated me, not like a son (that might have given offence) but like a long-lost friend. Blessings upon them! Once, too, in the Officers' Club at Arras where I was dining alone, and quite happy with my book and my wine (a bottle of Heidsieck then cost 8 francs, and a bottle of Perrier Jouet, 12) two immensely senior officers, all covered with ribbons and red tabs, came over to my table towards the end of the meal, and hailing me as 'Sunny Jim' carried me off to their own for brandy and cigars. They weren't drunk either; nor did they make me drunk. It was pure good will. And though exceptional, this was not so very exceptional. There were nasty people in the army; but memory fills those months with pleasant, transitory contacts. Every few days one seemed to meet a scholar, an original, a poet, a cheery buffoon, a raconteur, or at the least a man of good will.

Some time in the middle of that winter I had the good luck to fall sick with what the troops called 'trench fever' and the doctors PUO (Pyrexia, unknown origin) and was sent for a wholly delightful three weeks to hospital at Le Tréport. Perhaps I ought to have mentioned before that I had had a weak chest ever since childhood and had very early learned to make a minor illness one of the pleasures of life, even in peace-time. Now, as an alternative to the trenches, a bed and a book were 'very heaven'. The hospital was a converted hotel and we were two in a room. My first week was marred by the fact that one of the night nurses was conducting a furious love affair with my room-mate. I had too high a temperature to be embarrassed, but the human whisper is a very tedious and unmusical noise; especially at night. After that my fortune mended. The amorous man was sent elsewhere and replaced by a musical misogynist from Yorkshire, who on our second morning together said to me, 'Eh, lad, if we make beds ourselves dom b——s won't stay in room so long' (or words to that effect). Accordingly, we made our own beds every day, and every day when the two VAD's looked in they said, 'Oh, they've made their beds! Aren't these two good?' and rewarded us with their brightest smiles. I think they attributed our action to gallantry.

It was here that I first read a volume of Chesterton's essays. I had never heard of him and had no idea of what he stood for; nor can I quite understand why he made such an immediate conquest of me. It might have been expected that my pessimism, my atheism, and my hatred of sentiment would have made him to me the least congenial of all authors. It would almost seem that Providence, or some 'second cause' of a very obscure kind, quite over-rules our previous tastes when It decides to bring two minds together. Liking an author may be as involuntary and improbable as falling in love. I was by now a sufficiently experienced reader to distinguish liking from agreement. I did not need to accept what Chesterton said in order to enjoy it. His humour was of the kind which I like best— not 'jokes' imbedded in the page like currants in a cake, still less (what I cannot endure), a general tone of flippancy and jocularity, but the humour which is not in any way separable from the argument but is rather (as Aristotle would say) the 'bloom' on dialectic itself. The sword glitters not because the swordsman set out to make it glitter but because he is fighting for his life and therefore moving it very quickly. For the critics who think Chesterton frivolous or 'paradoxical' I have to work hard to feel even pity; sympathy is out of the question. Moreover, strange as it may seem, I liked him for his goodness. I can attribute this taste to myself freely (even at that age) because it was a liking for goodness which had nothing to do with any attempt to be good myself. I have never felt the dislike of goodness which seems to be quite common in better men than me. 'Smug' and 'smugness' were terms of disapprobation which had never had a place in my critical vocabulary. I lacked the cynic's nose, the *odora canum vis* or bloodhound sensitivity for hypocrisy or Pharisaism. It was a matter of taste: I felt the 'charm' of goodness as a man feels the charm of a woman he has no intention of marrying. It is, indeed, at that distance that its 'charm' is most apparent.

In reading Chesterton, as in reading MacDonald, I did not know what I was letting myself in for. A young man who wishes to remain a sound Atheist cannot be too careful of his reading. There are traps everywhere— 'Bibles laid open, millions of surprises,' as Herbert says, 'fine nets and stratagems.' God is, if I may say it, very unscrupulous.

In my own battalion also I was assailed. Here I met one Johnson (on whom be peace) who would have been a lifelong friend if he had not been killed. He was, like me, already a scholar of an Oxford college (Queen's) who hoped to take up his scholarship after the war, but a few years my senior and at that time in command of a company. In him I found dialectical sharpness such as I had hitherto known only in Kirk, but coupled with youth and whim and poetry. He was moving towards Theism and we had endless arguments on that and every other topic whenever we were out of the line. But it was not this that mattered. The important thing was that he was a man of conscience. I had hardly till now encountered principles in anyone so nearly of my own age and my own sort. The alarming thing was that he took them for granted. It crossed my mind for the first time since my apostasy that the severer virtues might have some relevance to one's own life. I say 'the severer virtues' because I already had some notion of kindness and faithfulness to friends and generosity about money—as who has not till he meets the temptation which gives all their opposite vices new and more civil names? But it had not seriously occurred to me that people like ourselves, people like Johnson and me who wanted to know whether beauty was objective or how Aeschylus handled the reconciliation of Zeus and

Prometheus, should be attempting strict veracity, chastity, or devotion to duty. I had taken it that they were not our subjects. There was no discussion between us on the point and I do not think he ever suspected the truth about me. I was at no pains to display it. If this is hypocrisy, then I must conclude that hypocrisy can do a man good. To be ashamed of what you were about to say, to pretend that something which you had meant seriously was only a joke—this is an ignoble part. But it is better than not to be ashamed at all. And the distinction between pretending you are better than you are and beginning to be better in reality is finer than moral sleuthhounds conceive. I was, in intention, concealing only a part: I accepted his principles at once, made no attempt internally to defend my own 'unexamined life'. When a boor first enters the society of courteous people what can he do, for a while, except imitate the motions? How can he learn except by imitation?

You will have divined that ours was a very nice battalion; a minority of good regulars ruling a pleasantly mixed population of promoted rankers (west country farmers, these), barristers, and university men. You could get as good talk there as anywhere. Perhaps the best of us all was our butt, Wallie. Wallie was a farmer, a Roman Catholic, a passionate soldier (the only man I met who really longed for fighting) and gullible to any degree by the rawest subaltern. The technique was to criticise the Yeomanry. Poor Wallie knew that it was the bravest, the most efficient, the hardest and cleanest corps that ever sat on horses. He knew all that inside, having learned it from an uncle in the Yeomanry when he was a child. But he could not get it out. He stammered and contradicted himself and always came at last to his trump card: 'I wish my Uncle Ben was here to talk to you. Uncle Ben'd talk to you. He'd tell you.' Mortals must not judge; but I doubt whether any man fought in France who was more likely to go straight to Heaven if he were killed. I would have been better employed cleaning his boots than laughing at him. I may add that I did not enjoy the short time I spent in the company he commanded. Wallie had a genuine passion for killing Germans and a complete disregard of his own or anyone else's safety. He was always striking out bright ideas at which the hair of us subalterns stood on end. Luckily he could be very easily dissuaded by any plausible argument that occurred to us. Such was his valour and innocence that he never for a moment suspected us of any but a military motive. He could never grasp the neighbourly principles which, by the tacit agreement of the troops, were held to govern trench-warfare, and to which I was introduced at once by my sergeant. I had suggested 'pooping' a rifle grenade into a German post where we had seen heads moving. 'Just as 'ee like, zir,' said the sergeant, scratching his head, 'but once 'ee start doing that kind of thing, 'ee'll get zummit back, zee?'

I must not paint the war-time army all gold. I met there both the World and the great goddess Nonsense. The world presented itself in a very ridiculous form on that night (my nineteenth birthday) when I first arrived 'up the line'. As I emerged from the shaft into the dug-out and blinked in the candle-light I noticed that the Captain to whom I was reporting was a master whom I had liked more than I had respected at one of my schools. I ventured to claim acquaintance. He admitted in a low, hurried voice that he had once been a schoolmaster, and the topic was never raised between us again. The impact of the Great Goddess was even funnier, and I met it long before I had reached my own battalion. The troop train from Rouen— that interminable, twelve-mile-an-hour train, in which no two coaches were alike—left at about ten in the evening. Three other officers and I were allotted a compartment. There was no heating; for light we brought our own candles; for sanitation there were the windows. The journey would last about fifteen hours. It was freezing hard. In the tunnel just outside Rouen (all my generation remember it) there was a sudden wrenching and grating noise and one of our doors dropped off bodily into the dark. We sat with chattering teeth till the next stop, where the officer commanding the train came bustling up and demanded what we had done with our door. 'It came off, sir,' said we. 'Don't talk nonsense,' said he, 'it wouldn't have come off if there hadn't been some horseplay!'—as if nothing were more natural than that four officers (being, of course, provided with screwdrivers) should begin a night journey in midwinter by removing the door of their carriage.

The war itself has been so often described by those who saw more of it than I that I shall say here little about it. Until the great German attack came in the Spring we had a pretty quiet time. Even then they attacked not us but the Canadians on our right, merely 'keeping us quiet' by pouring shells into our line about three a minute all day. I think it was that day I noticed how a great terror overcomes a less: a mouse that I met (and a poor shivering mouse it was, as I was a poor shivering man) made no attempt to run from me. Through the winter, weariness and water were our chief enemies. I have gone to sleep marching and woken again and found myself marching still. One walked in the trenches in thigh gum boots with water above the knee; one remembers the icy stream welling up inside the boot when you punctured it on concealed barbed wire. Familiarity both with the very old and the very recent dead confirmed that view of corpses which had been formed the moment I saw my dead mother. I came to know and pity and reverence the ordinary man: particularly dear Sergeant Ayres, who was (I suppose) killed by the same shell that wounded me. I was a futile officer (they gave commissions too easily then), a puppet moved about by him, and he turned this ridiculous and painful relation into something beautiful, became to me almost like a father. But for the rest, the war—the frights, the cold, the smell of H. E., the horribly smashed men still moving like half-crushed beetles, the sitting or standing corpses, the landscape of sheer earth without a blade of grass, the boots worn day and night till they seemed to grow to your feet—all this shows rarely and faintly in memory. It is too cut off from the rest of my experience and often seems to have happened to someone else. It is even in a way unimportant. One imaginative moment seems now to matter more than the realities that followed. It was the first bullet I heard—so far from me that it 'whined' like a journalist's or a peace-time poet's bullet. At that moment there was something not exactly like fear, much less like indifference: a little quavering signal that said, 'This is War. This is what Homer wrote about.'

XIII

THE NEW LOOK

This wall I was many a weary month in finishing,
and yet never thought myself safe till it was done.

DEFOE, *Robinson Crusoe*

The rest of my war experiences have little to do with this story. How I 'took' about sixty prisoners—that is, discovered to my great relief that the crowd of field-grey figures who suddenly appeared from nowhere, all had their hands up—is not worth telling, save as a joke. Did not Falstaff 'take' Sir Colville of the Dale? Nor does it concern the reader to know how I got a sound 'Blighty' from an English shell, or how the exquisite Sister N. in the CCS has ever since embodied my idea of Artemis. Two things stand out. One is the moment, just after I had been hit, when I found (or thought I found) that I was not breathing and concluded that this was death. I felt no fear and certainly no courage. It did not seem to be an occasion for either. The proposition 'Here is a man dying' stood before my mind as dry, as factual, as unemotional as something in a textbook. It was not even interesting. The fruit of this experience was that when, some years later, I met Kant's distinction between the Noumenal and the Phenomenal self, it was more to me than an abstraction. I had tasted it; I had proved that there was a fully conscious 'I' whose connections with the 'me' of introspection were loose and transitory. The other momentous experience was that of reading Bergson in a Convalescent Camp on Salisbury Plain. Intellectually this taught me to avoid the snares that lurk about the word *Nothing.* But it also had a revolutionary effect on my emotional outlook. Hitherto my whole bent had been towards things pale, remote, and evanescent; the watercolour world of Morris, the leafy recesses of Malory,[1] the twilight of Yeats. The word *life* had for me pretty much the same associations it had for Shelley in *The Triumph of Life.* I would not have understood what Goethe meant by *des Lebens goldnes Baum.* Bergson showed me. He did not abolish my old loves, but he gave me a new one. From him I first learned to relish energy, fertility, and urgency; the resource, the triumphs, and even the insolence, of things that grow. I became capable of appreciating artists who would, I believe,

---

[1] The iron in Malory, the tragedy of contrition, I did not yet at all perceive.

have meant nothing to me before; all the resonant, dog-
matic, flaming, unanswerable people like Beethoven, Titian
(in his mythological pictures), Goethe, Dunbar, Pindar,
Christopher Wren, and the more exultant Psalms.

I returned to Oxford—'demobbed'—in January 1919.
But before I say anything of my life there I must warn the
reader that one huge and complex episode will be omitted.
I have no choice about this reticence. All I can or need
say is that my earlier hostility to the emotions was very
fully and variously avenged. But even were I free to tell
the story, I doubt if it has much to do with the subject of
the book.

The first lifelong friend I made at Oxford was
A. K. Hamilton Jenkin, since known for his books on
Cornwall. He continued (what Arthur had begun) my
education as a seeing, listening, smelling, receptive creature. Arthur had had his preference for the Homely. But
Jenkin seemed to be able to enjoy everything; even ugliness. I learned from him that we should attempt a total
surrender to whatever atmosphere was offering itself at
the moment; in a squalid town to seek out those very
places where its squalor rose to grimness and almost
grandeur, on a dismal day to find the most dismal and
dripping wood, on a windy day to seek the windiest
ridge. There was no Betjemannic irony about it; only a

serious, yet gleeful, determination to rub one's nose in the very quiddity of each thing, to rejoice in its being (so magnificently) what it was.

My next was Owen Barfield. There is a sense in which Arthur and Barfield are the types of every man's First Friend and Second Friend. The First is the *alter ego,* the man who first reveals to you that you are not alone in the world by turning out (beyond hope) to share all your most secret delights. There is nothing to be overcome in making him your friend; he and you join like rain-drops on a window. But the Second Friend is the man who dis-agrees with you about everything. He is not so much the *alter ego* as the anti-self. Of course he shares your inter-ests; otherwise he would not become your friend at all. But he has approached them all at a different angle. He has read all the right books but has got the wrong thing out of every one. It is as if he spoke your language but mispronounced it. How can he be so nearly right and yet, invariably, just not right? He is as fascinating (and infuriating) as a woman. When you set out to correct his heresies, you find that he forsooth has decided to cor-rect yours! And then you go at it, hammer and tongs, far into the night, night after night, or walking through fine country that neither gives a glance to, each learning the weight of the other's punches, and often more like mutu-

ally respectful enemies than friends. Actually (though
it never seems so at the time) you modify one another's
thought; out of this perpetual dog-fight a community of
mind and a deep affection emerge. But I think he changed
me a good deal more than I him. Much of the thought
which he afterwards put into *Poetic Diction* had already
become mine before that important little book appeared.
It would be strange if it had not. He was of course not so
learned then as he has since become; but the genius was
already there.

Closely linked with Barfield of Wadham was his friend
(and soon mine), A. C. Harwood of The House, later a
pillar of Michael Hall, the Steinerite school at Kidbrooke.
He was different from either of us; a wholly imperturbable
man. Though poor (like most of us) and wholly without
'prospects', he wore the expression of a nineteenth-century
gentleman with something in the Funds. On a walking
tour when the last light of a wet evening had just revealed
some ghastly error in map-reading (probably his own)
and the best hope was 'Five miles to Mudham (if we could
find it) and we *might* get beds there,' he still wore that
expression. In the heat of argument he wore it still. You
would think that he, if anyone, would have been told to
'take that look off his face'. But I don't believe he ever
was. It was no mask and came from no stupidity. He has

been tried since by all the usual sorrows and anxieties. He is the sole Horatio known to me in this age of Hamlets; no 'stop for Fortune's finger'.

There is one thing to be said about these and other friends whom I made at Oxford. They were all, by decent Pagan standards (much more, by so low a standard as mine), 'good'. That is, they all, like my friend Johnson, believed, and acted on the belief, that veracity, public spirit, chastity, and sobriety were obligatory—'to be attempted', as the examiners say, 'by all candidates'. Johnson had prepared me to be influenced by them. I accepted their standards in principle and perhaps (this part I do not very well remember) tried to act accordingly.

During my first two years at Oxford I was busily engaged (apart from 'doing Mods' and 'beginning Greats') in assuming what we may call an intellectual 'New Look'. There was to be no more pessimism, no more self-pity, no flirtations with any idea of the supernatural, no romantic delusions. In a word, like the heroine of *Northanger Abbey,* I formed the resolution 'of always judging and acting in future with the greatest good sense'. And good sense meant, for me at that moment, a retreat, almost a panic-stricken flight, from all that sort of romanticism which had hitherto been the chief concern of my life. Several causes operated together.

For one thing, I had recently come to know an old, dirty, gabbling, tragic, Irish parson who had long since lost his faith but retained his living. By the time I met him his only interest was the search for evidence of 'human survival'. On this he read and talked incessantly, and, having a highly critical mind, could never satisfy himself. What was especially shocking was that the ravenous desire for personal immortality co-existed in him with (apparently) a total indifference to all that could, on a sane view, make immortality desirable. He was not seeking the Beatific Vision and did not even believe in God. He was not hoping for more time in which to purge and improve his own personality. He was not dreaming of reunion with dead friends or lovers; I never heard him speak with affection of anybody. All he wanted was the assurance that something he could call 'himself' would, on almost any terms, last longer than his bodily life. So, at least, I thought. I was too young and hard to suspect that what secretly moved him was a thirst for the happiness which had been wholly denied him on earth. And his state of mind appeared to me the most contemptible I had ever encountered. Any thoughts or dreams which might lead one into that fierce monomania were, I decided, to be utterly shunned. The whole question of immortality became rather disgusting to me. I shut it out. All one's thoughts must be confined to

the very world, which is the world
Of all of us—the place where, in the end,
We find our happiness, or not at all.

Secondly, it had been my chance to spend fourteen days, and most of the fourteen nights as well, in close contact with a man who was going mad. He was a man whom I had dearly loved, and well he deserved love. And now I helped to hold him while he kicked and wallowed on the floor, screaming out that devils were tearing him and that he was that moment falling down into Hell. And this man, as I well knew, had not kept the beaten track. He had flirted with Theosophy, Yoga, Spiritualism, Psychoanalysis, what not? Probably these things had in fact no connection with his insanity, for which (I believe) there were physical causes. But it did not seem so to me at the time. I thought I had seen a warning; it was to this, this raving on the floor, that all romantic longings and unearthly speculations led a man in the end—

Be not too wildly amorous of the far
Nor lure thy fantasy to its utmost scope.

Safety first, thought I: the beaten track, the approved road, the centre of the road, the lights on. For some months after that nightmare fortnight, the words *ordinary* and *humdrum* summed up everything that appeared to me most desirable.

Thirdly, the new Psychology was at that time sweeping through us all. We did not swallow it whole (few people then did) but we were all influenced. What we were most concerned about was 'Fantasy' or 'wishful thinking'. For (of course) we were all poets and critics and set a very great value on 'Imagination' in some high Coleridgean sense, so that it became important to distinguish Imagination, not only (as Coleridge did) from Fancy, but also from Fantasy as the psychologists understand that term. Now what, I asked myself, were all my delectable mountains and western gardens but sheer Fantasies? Had they not revealed their true nature by luring me, time and again, into undisguisedly erotic reverie or the squalid nightmare of Magic? In reality, of course, as previous chapters have told, my own experience had repeatedly shown that these romantic images had never been more than a sort of flash, or even slag, thrown off by the occurrence of Joy, that those mountains and gardens had never been what I wanted but only symbols which professed themselves to be no more, and that every effort to treat them as the real Desirable soon honestly proved itself to be a failure. But now, busy with my New Look, I managed to forget this. Instead of repenting my idolatry I vilified the unoffending images on which I had lavished it. With the confidence of a boy I decided I had done with all that. No more Avalon, no more Hesperides. I had (this was very precisely the opposite of the truth) 'seen through' them. And I was never going to be taken in again.

Finally, there was of course Bergson. Somehow or other (for it does not seem very clear when I re-open his books today) I found in him a refutation of the old haunting idea, Schopenhauer's idea, that the universe 'might not have existed'. In other words one Divine attribute, that of necessary existence, rose above my horizon. It was still, and long after, attached to the wrong subject; to the universe, not to God. But the mere attribute was itself of immense potency. When once one had dropped the absurd notion that reality is an arbitrary alternative to 'nothing', one gives up being a pessimist (or even an optimist). There is no sense in blaming or praising the Whole, nor, indeed, in saying anything about it. Even if you persist in hurling Promethean or Hardyesque defiances at it, then, since you are part of it, it is only that same Whole which through you 'quietly declaims the cursings of itself'—a futility which seems to me to vitiate Lord Russell's stirring essay on 'The Worship of a Free Man'. Cursings were as futile, and as immature, as dreams about the western garden. One must (like Carlyle's lady) 'accept' the universe; totally, with no reservations, loyally. This sort of Stoical Monism was the philosophy of my New Look. And it gave me a great sense of peace. It was perhaps the nearest thing to a religious experience which I had had since my prep. school days. It ended (I hope for ever) any idea of a treaty or compromise with reality. So much the perception of even one Divine attribute can do.

As for Joy, I labelled it 'aesthetic experience' and talked much about it under that name and said it was very 'valuable'. But it came very seldom and when it came it didn't amount to much.

Those early days of the New Look were on the whole happy ones. Very gradually the sky changed. There came to be more unhappiness and anxiety in my own life; and Barfield was living through

that whole year of youth
when life ached like an aching tooth.

Our generation, the generation of the returned soldiers, began to pass. Oxford was full of new faces. Freshmen began to make historical allowances for our warped point of view. The problem of one's career loomed larger and grimmer.

It was then that a really dreadful thing (dreadful to me) happened. First Harwood (still without changing his expression), and then Barfield, embraced the doctrines of Steiner and became Anthroposophists. I was hideously shocked. Everything that I had laboured so hard to expel from my own life seemed to have flared up and met me in my best friends. Not only my best friends, but those whom I would have thought safest; the one so immovable, the other brought up in a free-thinking family and so immune from all 'superstition' that he had hardly heard of Christianity itself until he went to school. (The gospel first broke on Barfield in the form of a dictated list of Parables Peculiar to St Matthew.) Not only in my seeming-safest friends but at a moment when we all had most need to stand together. And as I came to learn (so far as I ever have learned) what Steiner thought, my horror turned into disgust and resentment. For here, apparently, were all the abominations; none more abominable than those which had once attracted me. Here were gods, spirits, after-life and pre-existence, initiates, occult knowledge, meditation. 'Why—damn it—it's *medieval*,' I exclaimed; for I still had all the chronological snobbery of my period and used the names of earlier periods as terms of abuse. Here was everything which the New Look had been designed to exclude; everything that might lead one off the main road into those dark places where men wallow on the floor and scream that they are being dragged down into Hell. Of course it was all arrant nonsense. There was no danger of *my* being taken in. But then, the loneliness, the sense of being deserted.

Naturally, I attributed to my friends the same desires which, had I become an Anthroposophist, would have been operative in me. I thought they were falling under that ravenous, salt lust for the occult. I now see that, from the very first, all the evidence was against this. They were not that sort. Nor does Anthroposophy, so far as I can see, cater for that sort. There is a difficulty and (to me) a re-assuring Germanic dullness about it which would soon deter those who were looking for thrills. Nor have I ever seen that it had a deleterious effect on the character of those who embraced it; I have once known it to have a very good one.

I say this, not because I ever came within a hundred miles of accepting the thing myself, but in common fairness, and also as tardy amends for the many hard, unjust, and bitter things I once said about it to my friends. For Barfield's conversion to Anthroposophy marked the beginning of what I can only describe as the Great War between him and me. It was never, thank God, a quarrel, though it could have become one in a moment if he had used to me anything like the violence I allowed myself to him. But it was an almost incessant disputation, sometimes by letter and sometimes face to face, which lasted for years. And this Great War was one of the turning points of my life.

Barfield never made me an Anthroposophist, but his counter-attacks destroyed for ever two elements in my own thought. In the first place he made short work of what I have called my 'chronological snobbery', the uncritical acceptance of the intellectual climate common to our own age and the assumption that whatever has gone out of date is on that account discredited. You must find why it went out of date. Was it ever refuted (and if so by whom, where, and how conclusively) or did it merely die away as fashions do? If the latter, this tells us nothing about its truth or falsehood. From seeing this, one passes to the realisation that our own age is also 'a period', and certainly has, like all periods, its own characteristic illusions. They are likeliest to lurk in those widespread assumptions which are so ingrained in the age that no one dares to attack or feels it necessary to defend them. In the second place he convinced me that the positions we had hitherto held left no room for any satisfactory theory of knowledge. We had been, in the technical sense of the term, 'realists'; that is, we accepted as rock-bottom reality the universe

revealed by the senses. But at the same time we continued
to make for certain phenomena of consciousness all the
claims that really went with a theistic or idealistic view.
We maintained that abstract thought (if obedient to logical rules) gave indisputable truth, that our moral judgement was 'valid', and our aesthetic experience not merely
pleasing but 'valuable'. The view was, I think, common
at the time; it runs through Bridges' *Testament of Beauty*,
the work of Gilbert Murray, and Lord Russell's 'Worship
of a Free Man'. Barfield convinced me that it was incon-
sistent. If thought were a purely subjective event, these
claims for it would have to be abandoned. If one kept (as
rock-bottom reality) the universe of the senses, aided by
instruments and co-ordinated so as to form 'science', then
one would have to go much further—as many have since
gone—and adopt a Behaviouristic theory of logic, ethics,
and aesthetics. But such a theory was, and is, unbelievable to me. I am using the word 'unbelievable', which
many use to mean 'improbable' or even 'undesirable', in
a quite literal sense. I mean that the act of believing what
the behaviourist believes is one that my mind simply will
not perform. I cannot force my thought into that shape
any more than I can scratch my ear with my big toe or
pour wine out of a bottle into the cavity at the base of that
same bottle. It is as final as a physical impossibility. I was

therefore compelled to give up realism. I had been trying to defend it ever since I began reading philosophy. Partly, no doubt, this was mere 'cussedness'. Idealism was then the dominant philosophy at Oxford and I was by nature 'against Government'. But partly, too, realism satisfied an emotional need. I wanted Nature to be quite independent of our observation; something other, indifferent, self-existing. (This went with the Jenkinian zest for rubbing one's nose in the mere quiddity.) But now, it seemed to me, I had to give that up. Unless I were to accept an unbelievable alternative, I must admit that mind was no late-come epiphenomenon; that the whole universe was, in the last resort, mental; that our logic was participation in a cosmic *Logos*.

It is astonishing (at this time of day) that I could regard this position as something quite distinct from Theism. I suspect there was some wilful blindness. But there were in those days all sorts of blankets, insulators, and insurances which enabled one to get all the conveniences of Theism, without believing in God. The English Hegelians, writers like T. H. Green, Bradley, and Bosanquet (then mighty names), dealt in precisely such wares. The Absolute Mind—better still, the Absolute—was impersonal, or it knew itself (but not us?) only in us, and it was so absolute that it wasn't really much more like a mind than anything else. And anyway, the more muddled one got about it and the more contradictions one committed, the more this proved that our discursive thought moved only on the level of 'Appearance', and 'Reality' must be somewhere else. And where else but, of course, in the Absolute? There, not here, was 'the fuller splendour' behind the 'sensuous curtain'. The emotion that went with all this was certainly religious. But this was a religion that cost nothing. We could talk religiously about the Absolute; but there was no danger of Its doing anything about us. It was 'there'; safely and immovably 'there'. It would never come 'here', never (to be blunt) make a nuisance of Itself. This quasi-religion was all a one-way street; all *eros* (as Dr Nygren would say) steaming up, but no *agape* darting down. There was nothing to fear; better still, nothing to obey.

Yet there was one really wholesome element in it. The Absolute was 'there', and that 'there' contained the reconciliation of all contraries, the transcendence of all finitude, the hidden glory which was the only perfectly real thing there is. In fact, it had much of the quality of Heaven. But it was a Heaven none of us could ever get to. For we are appearances. To be 'there' is, by definition, not to be we. All who embrace such a philosophy live, like Dante's virtuous Pagans, 'in desire without hope'. Or like Spinoza they so love their God as to be unable even to wish that

He should love them in return. I should be very sorry not to have passed through that experience. I think it is more religious than many experiences that have been called Christian. What I learned from the Idealists (and still most strongly hold) is this maxim: it is more important that Heaven should exist than that any of us should reach it.

And so the great Angler played His fish and I never dreamed that the hook was in my tongue. But two great advances had been made. Bergson had showed me necessary existence; and from Idealism I had come one step nearer to understanding the words, 'We give thanks to thee for thy great glory.' The Norse gods had given me the first hint of it; but then I didn't believe in them, and I did believe (so far as one can believe an *Unding*) in the Absolute.

XIV

CHECKMATE

The one principle of hell is—'I am my own.'

GEORGE MACDONALD

In the summer of 1922 I finished Greats. As there were no philosophical posts going, or none that I could get, my long-suffering father offered me a fourth year at Oxford during which I read English so as to get a second string to my bow. The Great War with Barfield had, I think, begun at this time.

No sooner had I entered the English School than I went to George Gordon's discussion class. And there I made a new friend. The very first words he spoke marked him out from the ten or twelve others who were present; a man after my own heart, and that too at an age when the instantaneous friendships of earlier youth were becoming rather rare events. His name was Nevill Coghill. I soon had the shock of discovering that he—clearly the most intelligent and best-informed man in that class—was a Christian and a thoroughgoing supernaturalist. There were other traits that I liked but found (for I was still very much a modern) oddly archaic; chivalry, honour, courtesy, 'freedom', and 'gentillesse'. One could imagine him fighting a duel. He spoke much 'ribaldry' but never 'villeinye'. Barfield was beginning to overthrow my chronological snobbery; Coghill gave it another blow. Had something really dropped out of our lives? Was the archaic simply the civilised, and the modern simply the barbaric? It will seem strange to many of my critics who regard me as a typical *laudator temporis acti* that this question should have arisen so comparatively late in my life. But then the key to my books is Donne's maxim, 'The heresies that men leave are hated most.' The things I assert most vigorously are those that I resisted long and accepted late.

These disturbing factors in Coghill ranged themselves with a wider disturbance which was now threatening my whole earlier outlook. All the books were beginning to turn against me. Indeed, I must have been as blind as a bat not to have seen, long before, the ludicrous contradiction between my theory of life and my actual experiences as a reader. George MacDonald had done more to me than any other writer; of course it was a pity he had that bee in his bonnet about Christianity. He was good *in spite of it*. Chesterton had more sense than all the other moderns put together; bating, of course, his Christianity. Johnson was one of the few authors whom I felt I could trust utterly; curiously enough, he had the same kink. Spenser and Milton by a strange coincidence had it too. Even among ancient authors the same paradox was to be found. The most religious (Plato, Aeschylus, Virgil) were clearly those on whom I could really feed. On the other hand, those writers who did not suffer from religion and with whom in theory my sympathy ought to have been complete—Shaw and Wells and Mill and Gibbon and Voltaire—all seemed a little thin; what as boys we called 'tinny'. It wasn't that I didn't like them. They were all (especially Gibbon) entertaining; but hardly more. There seemed to be no depth in them. They were too simple. The roughness and density of life did not appear in their books.

Now that I was reading more English, the paradox began to be aggravated. I was deeply moved by the *Dream of the Rood;* more deeply still by Langland; intoxicated (for a time) by Donne; deeply and lastingly satisfied by Thomas Browne. But the most alarming of all was George Herbert. Here was a man who seemed to me to excel all the authors I had ever read in conveying the very quality of life as we actually live it from moment to moment; but the wretched fellow, instead of doing it all directly, insisted on mediating it through what I would still have called 'the

Christian mythology'. On the other hand most of the authors who might be claimed as precursors of modern enlightenment seemed to me very small beer and bored me cruelly. I thought Bacon (to speak frankly) a solemn, pretentious ass, yawned my way through Restoration Comedy, and, having manfully struggled on to the last line of *Don Juan*, wrote on the end-leaf 'Never again'. The only non-Christians who seemed to me really to know anything were the Romantics; and a good many of them were dangerously tinged with something like religion, even at times with Christianity. The upshot of it all could nearly be expressed in a perversion of Roland's great line in the *Chanson*—

Christians are wrong, but all the rest are bores.

The natural step would have been to enquire a little more closely whether the Christians were, after all, wrong. But I did not take it. I thought I could explain their superiority without that hypothesis. Absurdly (yet many Absolute Idealists have shared this absurdity) I thought that 'the Christian myth' conveyed to unphilosophic minds as much of the truth, that is of Absolute Idealism, as they were capable of grasping, and that even that much put them above the irreligious. Those who could not rise to the notion of the Absolute would come nearer to the truth by belief in 'a God' than by disbelief. Those who could not understand how, as Reasoners, we participated in a timeless and therefore deathless world, would get a symbolic shadow of the truth by believing in a life after death. The implication—that something which I and most other undergraduates could master without extraordinary pains would have been too hard for Plato, Dante, Hooker, and Pascal—did not yet strike me as absurd. I hope this is because I never looked it squarely in the face.

As the plot quickens and thickens towards its end, I leave out more and more of such matters as would go into a full autobiography. My father's death, with all the fortitude (even playfulness) which he displayed in his last illness, does not really come into the story I am telling. My brother was at that time in Shanghai. Nor would it be relevant to tell in detail how I became a temporary lecturer at Univ. for a year and was elected a fellow of Magdalen in 1925. The worst is that I must leave undescribed many men whom I love and to whom I am deeply in debt: G. H. Stevenson and E. F. Carritt, my tutors, the Fark (but who could paint him anyway?), and five great Magdalen men who enlarged my very idea of what a learned life should be—P. V. M. Benecke, C. C. J. Webb, J. A. Smith, F. E. Brightman, and C. T. Onions. Except for Oldie, I have always been blessed both in my official and my unofficial teachers. In my earlier years at Magdalen I inhabited a world where hardly anything I wanted to know needed to be found out by my own unaided efforts. One or other of these could always give you a clue. ('You'll find something about it in Alanus . . .'—'Macrobius would be the man to try . . .'—'Doesn't Comparetti mention it?'—'Have you looked for it in Du Cange?') I found, as always, that the ripest are kindest to the raw and the most studious have most time to spare. When I began teaching for the English Faculty, I made two other friends, both Christians (these queer people seemed now to pop up on every side) who were later to give me much help in getting over the last stile. They were H. V. D. Dyson (then of Reading) and J. R. R. Tolkien. Friendship with the latter marked the breakdown of two old prejudices. At my first coming into the world I had been (implicitly) warned never to trust a Papist, and at my first coming into the English Faculty (explicitly) never to trust a philologist. Tolkien was both.

Realism had been abandoned; the New Look was somewhat damaged; and chronological snobbery was seriously shaken. All over the board my pieces were in the most disadvantageous positions. Soon I could no longer cherish even the illusion that the initiative lay with me. My Adversary began to make His final moves.

The first Move annihilated the last remains of the New Look. I was suddenly impelled to re-read (which was certainly no business of mine at the moment) the *Hippolytus* of Euripides. In one chorus all that world's end imagery which I had rejected when I assumed my New Look rose before me. I liked, but did not yield; I tried to patronise it. But next day I was overwhelmed. There was a transitional moment of delicious uneasiness, and then—instantaneously—the long inhibition was over, the dry desert lay behind, I was off once more into the land of longing, my heart at once broken and exalted as it had never been since the old days at Bookham. There was nothing whatever to do about it, no question of returning to the desert. I had simply been ordered—or, rather, compelled—to 'take that look off my face'. And never to resume it either.

The next Move was intellectual, and consolidated the first Move. I read in Alexander's *Space, Time, and Deity* his theory of 'Enjoyment' and 'Contemplation'. These are technical terms in Alexander's philosophy; 'Enjoyment' has nothing to do with pleasure, nor 'Contemplation' with the contemplative life. When you see a table you 'enjoy' the act of seeing and 'contemplate' the table. Later, if you took up Optics and thought about Seeing itself, you would be contemplating the seeing and enjoying the thought. In bereavement you contemplate the beloved and the beloved's death and, in Alexander's sense, 'enjoy' the loneliness and grief; but a psychologist, if he were considering you as a case of melancholia, would be contemplating your grief and enjoying psychology. We do not 'think a thought' in the same sense in which we 'think that Herodotus is unreliable'. When we think a thought, 'thought' is a cognate accusative (like 'blow' in 'strike a blow'). We enjoy the thought (that Herodotus is unreliable) and, in so doing, contemplate the unreliability of Herodotus.

I accepted this distinction at once and have ever since regarded it as an indispensable tool of thought. A moment later its consequences—for me quite catastrophic—began to appear. It seemed to me self-evident that one essential property of love, hate, fear, hope, or desire was attention to their object. To cease thinking about or attending to the woman is, so far, to cease loving; to cease thinking about or attending to the dreaded thing is, so far, to cease being afraid. But to attend to your own love or fear is to cease attending to the loved or dreaded object. In other words the enjoyment and the contemplation of our inner activities are incompatible. You cannot hope and also think about hoping at the same moment; for in hope we look to hope's object and we interrupt this by (so to speak) turning round to look at the hope itself. Of course the two activities can and do alternate with great rapidity; but they are distinct and incompatible. This was not merely a logical result of Alexander's analysis, but could be verified in daily and hourly experience. The surest means of disarming an anger or a lust was to turn your attention from the girl or the insult and start examining the passion itself. The surest way of spoiling a pleasure was to start examining your satisfaction. But if so, it followed that all introspection is in one respect misleading. In introspection we try to look 'inside ourselves' and see what is going on. But nearly everything that was going on a moment before is stopped by the very act of our turning to look at it. Unfortunately this does not mean that introspection finds nothing. On the contrary, it finds precisely what is left behind by the suspension of all our normal activities; and what is left behind is mainly mental images and physical sensations. The great error is to mistake this mere sediment or track or by-product for the activities themselves. That is how men may come to believe that thought is only unspoken words, or the appreciation of poetry only a collection of mental pictures, when these in reality are what the thought or the appreciation, when interrupted, leave behind—like the swell at sea, working after the wind has dropped. Not, of course, that these activities, before we stopped them by introspection, were unconscious. We do not love, fear, or think without knowing it. Instead of the twofold division into Conscious and Unconscious, we need a threefold division: the Unconscious, the Enjoyed, and the Contemplated.

This discovery flashed a new light back on my whole life. I saw that all my waitings and watchings for Joy, all my vain hopes to find some mental content on which I could, so to speak, lay my finger and say, 'This is it,' had been a futile attempt to contemplate the enjoyed. All that such watching and waiting ever *could* find would be either an image (Asgard, the western garden, or what not) or a quiver in the diaphragm. I should never have to bother again about these images or sensations. I knew now that they were merely the mental track left by the passage of Joy—not the wave but the wave's imprint on the sand. The inherent dialectic of desire itself had in a way already shown me this; for all images and sensations, if idolatrously mistaken for Joy itself, soon honestly confessed themselves inadequate. All said, in the last resort, 'It is not I. I am only a reminder. Look! Look! What do I remind you of?'

So far, so good. But it is at the next step that awe overtakes me. There was no doubt that Joy was a desire (and, in so far as it was also simultaneously a good, it was also a kind of love). But a desire is turned not to itself but to its object. Not only that, but it owes all its character to its object. Erotic love is not like desire for food, nay, a love for one woman differs from a love for another woman in the very same way and the very same degree as the two women differ from one another. Even our desire for one wine differs in tone from our desire for another. Our intellectual desire (curiosity) to know the true answer to a question is quite different from our desire to find that one answer, rather than another, is true. The form of the desired is in the desire. It is the object which makes the desire harsh or sweet, coarse or choice, 'high' or 'low'. It is the object that makes the desire itself desirable or hateful. I perceived (and this was a wonder of wonders) that just as I had been wrong in supposing that I really desired the Garden of the Hesperides, so also I had been equally wrong in supposing that I desired Joy itself. Joy itself, considered simply as an event in my own mind, turned out to be of no value at all. All the value lay in that of which Joy was the desiring. And that object, quite clearly, was no state of my own mind or body at all. In a way, I had proved this by elimination. I had tried every-thing in my own mind and body; as it were, asking myself 'Is it this you want? Is it this?' Last of all I had asked if Joy itself was what I wanted; and, labelling it 'aesthetic experience', had pretended I could answer Yes. But that answer too had broken down. Inexorably Joy proclaimed, 'You want—I myself am your want of—something other, outside, not you nor any state of you.' I did not yet ask, Who is the desired? only What is it? But this brought me already into the region of awe, for I thus understood that in deepest solitude there is a road right out of the self, a commerce with something which, by refusing to identify itself with any object of the senses, or anything whereof we have biological or social need, or anything imagined, or any state of our own minds, proclaims itself sheerly objective. Far more objective than bodies, for it is not, like them, clothed in our senses; the naked Other, image-less (though our imagination salutes it with a hundred images), unknown, undefined, desired.

That was the second Move; equivalent, perhaps, to the loss of one's last remaining bishop. The third Move did not seem to me dangerous at the time. It consisted merely in linking up this new *éclaircissement* about Joy with my idealistic philosophy. I saw that Joy, as I now understood it, would fit in. We mortals, seen as the sciences see us and as we commonly see one another, are mere 'appearances'. But appearances of the Absolute. In so far as we really are at all (which isn't saying much) we have, so to speak, a root in the Absolute, which is the utter reality.

And that is why we experience Joy: we yearn, rightly, for that unity which we can never reach except by ceasing to be the separate phenomenal beings called 'we'. Joy was not a deception. Its visitations were rather the moments of clearest consciousness we had, when we became aware of our fragmentary and phantasmal nature and ached for that impossible reunion which would annihilate us or that self-contradictory waking which would reveal, not that we had had, but that we *were,* a dream. This seemed quite satisfactory intellectually. Even emotionally too; for it matters more that Heaven should exist than that we should ever get there. What I did not notice was that I had passed an important milestone. Up till now my thoughts had been centrifugal; now the centripetal movement had begun. Considerations arising from quite different parts of my experience were beginning to come together with a click. This new dovetailing of my desire-life with my philosophy foreshadowed the day, now fast approaching, when I should be forced to take my 'philosophy' more seriously than I ever intended. I did not foresee this. I was like a man who has lost 'merely a pawn' and never dreams that this (in that state of the game) means mate in a few moves.

The fourth Move was more alarming. I was now teaching philosophy (I suspect very badly) as well as English.

And my watered Hegelianism wouldn't serve for tutorial purposes.[1] A tutor must make things clear. Now the Absolute cannot be made clear. Do you mean Nobody-knows-what, or do you mean a superhuman mind and therefore (we may as well admit) a Person? After all, did Hegel and Bradley and all the rest of them ever do more than add mystifications to the simple, workable, theistic idealism of Berkeley? I thought not. And didn't Berkeley's 'God' do all the same work as the Absolute, with the added advantage that we had at least some notion of what we meant by Him? I thought He did. So I was driven back into something like Berkeleyanism; but Berkeleyanism with a few top-dressings of my own. I distinguished this philosophical 'God' very sharply (or so I said) from 'the God of popular religion'. There was, I explained, no possibility of being in a personal relation with Him. For I thought He projected us as a dramatist projects his characters, and I could no more 'meet' Him, than Hamlet could meet Shakespeare. I didn't call Him 'God' either; I called Him 'Spirit'. One fights for one's remaining comforts.

Then I read Chesterton's *Everlasting Man* and for the

---

[1] Not, of course, that I thought it a tutor's business to make converts to his own philosophy. But I found I needed a position of my own as a basis from which to criticise my pupils' essays.

first time saw the whole Christian outline of history set out in a form that seemed to me to make sense. Somehow I contrived not to be too badly shaken. You will remember that I already thought Chesterton the most sensible man alive 'apart from his Christianity'. Now, I veritably believe, I thought—I didn't of course *say;* words would have revealed the nonsense—that Christianity itself was very sensible 'apart from its Christianity'. But I hardly remember, for I had not long finished *The Everlasting Man* when something far more alarming happened to me. Early in 1926 the hardest boiled of all the atheists I ever knew sat in my room on the other side of the fire and remarked that the evidence for the historicity of the Gospels was really surprisingly good. 'Rum thing,' he went on. 'All that stuff of Frazer's about the Dying God. Rum thing. It almost looks as if it had really happened once.' To understand the shattering impact of it, you would need to know the man (who has certainly never since shown any interest in Christianity). If he, the cynic of cynics, the toughest of toughs, were not—as I would still have put it—'safe', where could I turn? Was there then no escape?

The odd thing was that before God closed in on me, I was in fact offered what now appears a moment of wholly free choice. In a sense. I was going up Headington Hill on the top of a bus. Without words and (I think) almost without images, a fact about myself was somehow presented to me. I became aware that I was holding something at bay, or shutting something out. Or, if you like, that I was wearing some stiff clothing, like corsets, or even a suit of armour, as if I were a lobster. I felt myself being, there and then, given a free choice. I could open the door or keep it shut; I could unbuckle the armour or keep it on. Neither choice was presented as a duty; no threat or promise was attached to either, though I knew that to open the door or to take off the corslet meant the incalculable. The choice appeared to be momentous but it was also strangely unemotional. I was moved by no desires or fears. In a sense I was not moved by anything. I chose to open, to unbuckle, to loosen the rein. I say, 'I chose', yet it did not really seem possible to do the opposite. On the other hand, I was aware of no motives. You could argue that I was not a free agent, but I am more inclined to think that this came nearer to being a perfectly free act than most that I have ever done. Necessity may not be the opposite of freedom, and perhaps a man is most free when, instead of producing motives, he could only say, 'I am what I do.' Then came the repercussion on the imaginative level. I felt as if I were a man of snow at long last beginning to melt. The melting was starting in my back—drip-drip and presently trickle-trickle. I rather disliked the feeling.

The fox had been dislodged from Hegelian Wood and was now running in the open, 'with all the wo in the world', bedraggled and weary, hounds barely a field behind. And nearly everyone now (one way or another) in the pack; Plato, Dante, MacDonald, Herbert, Barfield, Tolkien, Dyson, Joy itself. Everyone and everything had joined the other side. Even my own pupil Griffiths—now Dom Bede Griffiths—though not yet himself a believer, did his share. Once, when he and Barfield were lunching in my room, I happened to refer to philosophy as 'a subject'. 'It wasn't a *subject* to Plato,' said Barfield, 'it was a way.' The quiet but fervent agreement of Griffiths, and the quick glance of understanding between these two, revealed to me my own frivolity. Enough had been thought, and said, and felt, and imagined. It was about time that something should be done.

For of course there had long been an ethic (theoretically) attached to my Idealism. I thought the business of us finite and half-unreal souls was to multiply the consciousness of Spirit by seeing the world from different positions while yet remaining qualitatively the same as Spirit; to be tied to a particular time and place and set of circumstances, yet there to will and think as Spirit itself does. This was hard; for the very act whereby Spirit projected souls and a world gave those souls different and competitive interests, so that there was a temptation to selfishness. But I thought each of us had it in his power to discount the emotional perspective produced by his own particular selfhood, just as we discount the optical perspective produced by our position in space. To prefer my own happiness to my neighbour's was like thinking that the nearest telegraph post was really the largest. The way to recover, and act upon, this universal and objective vision was daily and hourly to remember our true nature, to reascend or return into that Spirit which, in so far as we really were at all, we still were. Yes: but I now felt I had better try to do it. I faced at last (in MacDonald's words) 'something to be neither more nor less nor other than *done*'. An attempt at complete virtue must be made.

Really, a young Atheist cannot guard his faith too carefully. Dangers lie in wait for him on every side. You must not do, you must not even try to do, the will of the Father unless you are prepared to 'know of the doctrine'. All my acts, desires, and thoughts were to be brought into harmony with universal Spirit. For the first time I examined myself with a seriously practical purpose. And there I found what appalled me; a zoo of lusts, a bedlam of ambitions, a nursery of fears, a harem of fondled hatreds. My name was legion.

Of course I could do nothing—I could not last out

one hour—without continual conscious recourse to
what I called Spirit. But the fine, philosophical distinction between this and what ordinary people call 'prayer to
God' breaks down as soon as you start doing it in earnest.
Idealism can be talked, and even felt; it cannot be lived.
It became patently absurd to go on thinking of 'Spirit' as
either ignorant of, or passive to, my approaches. Even if
my own philosophy were true, how could the initiative
lie on my side? My own analogy, as I now first perceived,
suggested the opposite: if Shakespeare and Hamlet could
ever meet, it must be Shakespeare's doing.[2] Hamlet could
initiate nothing. Perhaps, even now, my Absolute Spirit
still differed in some way from the God of religion. The
real issue was not, or not yet, there. The real terror was
that if you seriously believed in even such a 'God' or
'Spirit' as I admitted, a wholly new situation developed.
As the dry bones shook and came together in that dreadful valley of Ezekiel's, so now a philosophical theorem,
cerebrally entertained, began to stir and heave and throw
off its gravecloths, and stood upright and became a living
presence. I was to be allowed to play at philosophy no

---

[2] i.e., Shakespeare could, in principle, make himself appear as Author
within the play, and write a dialogue between Hamlet and himself. The
'Shakespeare' within the play would of course be at once Shakespeare
and one of Shakespeare's creatures. It would bear some analogy to
Incarnation.

longer. It might, as I say, still be true that my 'Spirit' differed in some way from 'the God of popular religion'. My
Adversary waived the point. It sank into utter unimportance. He would not argue about it. He only said, 'I am
the Lord'; 'I am that I am'; 'I am.'

People who are naturally religious find difficulty in
understanding the horror of such a revelation. Amiable
agnostics will talk cheerfully about 'man's search for
God'. To me, as I then was, they might as well have talked
about the mouse's search for the cat. The best image of my
predicament is the meeting of Mime and Wotan in the first
act of *Siegfried; hier brauch' ich nicht Spärer noch Späher,
Einsam will ich* . . . (I've no use for spies and snoopers. I
would be private. . . .)

Remember, I had always wanted, above all things, not
to be 'interfered with'. I had wanted (mad wish) 'to call
my soul my own'. I had been far more anxious to avoid
suffering than to achieve delight. I had always aimed at
limited liabilities. The supernatural itself had been to me,
first, an illicit dram, and then, as by a drunkard's reaction,
nauseous. Even my recent attempt to live my philosophy
had secretly (I now knew) been hedged round by all sorts
of reservations. I had pretty well known that my ideal of
virtue would never be allowed to lead me into anything
intolerably painful; I would be 'reasonable'. But now what

had been an ideal became a command; and what might not be expected of one? Doubtless, by definition, God was Reason itself. But would He also be 'reasonable' in that other, more comfortable, sense? Not the slightest assurance on that score was offered me. Total surrender, the absolute leap in the dark, was demanded. The reality with which no treaty can be made was upon me. The demand was not even 'All or nothing'. I think that stage had been passed, on the bus-top when I unbuckled my armour and the snow-man started to melt. Now, the demand was simply 'All'.

You must picture me alone in that room at Magdalen, night after night, feeling, whenever my mind lifted even for a second from my work, the steady, unrelenting approach of Him whom I so earnestly desired not to meet. That which I greatly feared had at last come upon me. In the Trinity Term of 1929 I gave in, and admitted that God was God, and knelt and prayed: perhaps, that night, the most dejected and reluctant convert in all England. I did not then see what is now the most shining and obvious thing; the Divine humility which will accept a convert even on such terms. The Prodigal Son at least walked home on his own feet. But who can duly adore that Love which will open the high gates to a prodigal who is brought in kicking, struggling, resentful, and darting his eyes in every direction for a chance of escape? The words *compelle intrare*, compel them to come in, have been so abused by wicked men that we shudder at them; but, properly understood, they plumb the depth of the Divine mercy. The hardness of God is kinder than the softness of men, and His compulsion is our liberation.

XV

THE BEGINNING

Aliud est de silvestri cacumine videre patriam
pacis . . . et aliud tenere viam illuc ducentem.
ST AUGUSTINE, *Confessions,* VII, xxi

For it is one thing to see the land of peace from a
wooded ridge . . . and another to tread the road that
leads to it.

It must be understood that the conversion recorded in the
last chapter was only to Theism, pure and simple, not to
Christianity. I knew nothing yet about the Incarnation.
The God to whom I surrendered was sheerly non-human.

It may be asked whether my terror was at all relieved by
the thought that I was now approaching the source from
which those arrows of Joy had been shot at me ever since
childhood. Not in the least. No slightest hint was vouch-
safed me that there ever had been or ever would be any
connection between God and Joy. If anything, it was the

reverse. I had hoped that the heart of reality might be of such a kind that we can best symbolise it as a place; instead, I found it to be a Person. For all I knew, the total rejection of what I called Joy might be one of the demands, might be the very first demand He would make upon me. There was no strain of music from within, no smell of eternal orchards at the threshold, when I was dragged through the doorway. No kind of desire was present at all.

My conversion involved as yet no belief in a future life. I now number it among my greatest mercies that I was permitted for several months, perhaps for a year, to know God and to attempt obedience without even raising that question. My training was like that of the Jews to whom He revealed Himself centuries before there was a whisper of anything better (or worse) beyond the grave than shadowy and featureless *Sheol*. And I did not dream even of that. There are men, far better men than I, who have made immortality almost the central doctrine of their religion; but for my own part I have never seen how a preoccupation with that subject at the outset could fail to corrupt the whole thing. I had been brought up to believe that goodness was goodness only if it were disinterested, and that any hope of reward or fear of punishment contaminated the will. If I was wrong in this (the question is really much more complicated than I then perceived) my error was most tenderly allowed for. I was afraid that threats or promises would demoralise me; no threats or promises were made. The commands were inexorable, but they were backed by no 'sanctions'. God was to be obeyed simply because He was God. Long since, through the gods of Asgard, and later through the notion of the Absolute, He had taught me how a thing can be revered not for what it can do to us but for what it is in itself. That is why, though it was a terror, it was no surprise to learn that God is to be obeyed because of what He is in Himself. If you ask why we should obey God, in the last resort the answer is, 'I am.' To know God is to know that our obedience is due to Him. In His nature His sovereignty *de jure* is revealed.

Of course as I have said, the matter is more complicated than that. The primal and necessary Being, the Creator, has sovereignty *de facto* as well as *de jure*. He has the power as well as the kingdom and the glory. But the *de jure* sovereignty was made known to me before the power, the right before the might. And for this I am thankful. I think it is well, even now, sometimes to say to ourselves, 'God is such that if (*per impossibile*) His power could vanish and His other attributes remain, so that the supreme right were for ever robbed of the supreme might, we should still owe Him precisely the same kind and degree of allegiance as we now do.' On the other hand, while it is true to say that

God's own nature is the real sanction of His commands, yet to understand this must, in the end, lead us to the conclusion that union with that Nature is bliss and separation from it horror. Thus Heaven and Hell come in. But it may well be that to think much of either except in this context of thought, to hypostatise them as if they had a substantial meaning apart from the presence or absence of God, corrupts the doctrine of both and corrupts us while we so think of them.

The last stage in my story, the transition from mere Theism to Christianity, is the one on which I am now least informed. Since it is also the most recent, this ignorance may seem strange. I think there are two reasons. One is that as we grow older we remember the more distant past better than what is nearer. But the other is, I believe, that one of the first results of my Theistic conversion was a marked decrease (and high time, as all readers of this book will agree) in the fussy attentiveness which I had so long paid to the progress of my own opinions and the states of my own mind. For many healthy extroverts self-examination first begins with conversion. For me it was almost the other way round. Self-examination did of course continue. But it was (I suppose, for I cannot quite remember) at stated intervals, and for a practical purpose; a duty, a discipline, an uncomfortable thing, no longer a hobby or a habit. To believe and to pray were the beginning of extroversion. I had been, as they say, 'taken out of myself'. If Theism had done nothing else for me, I should still be thankful that it cured me of the time-wasting and foolish practice of keeping a diary. (Even for autobiographical purposes a diary is nothing like so useful as I had hoped. You put down each day what you think important; but of course you cannot each day see what will prove to have been important in the long run.[1])

As soon as I became a Theist I started attending my parish church on Sundays and my college chapel on weekdays; not because I believed in Christianity, nor because I thought the difference between it and simple Theism a small one, but because I thought one ought to 'fly one's flag' by some unmistakable overt sign. I was acting in obedience to a (perhaps mistaken) sense of honour. The idea of churchmanship was to me wholly unattractive. I was not in the least anti-clerical, but I was deeply anti-ecclesiastical. That curates and archdeacons and church-wardens should exist, was admirable. They gratified my

---

[1] The only real good I got from keeping a diary was that it taught me a just appreciation of Boswell's amazing genius. I tried very hard to reproduce conversations, in some of which very amusing and striking people had taken part. But none of these people came to life in the diary at all. Obviously something quite different from mere accurate reporting went to the presentation of Boswell's Langton, Beauclerk, Wilkes, and the rest.

Jenkinian love of everything which has its own strong flavour. And (apart from Oldie) I had been fortunate in my clerical acquaintances; especially in Adam Fox, the Dean of Divinity at Magdalen, and in Arthur Barton (later Archbishop of Dublin) who had been our Rector at home in Ireland. (He, by the by, had once suffered under Oldie at Belsen. Speaking of Oldie's death, I had said to him, 'Well, we shan't see *him* again.' 'You mean,' he answered with a grim smile, 'we *hope* we shan't.') But though I liked clergymen as I liked bears, I had as little wish to be in the Church as in the zoo. It was, to begin with, a kind of collective; a wearisome 'get-together' affair. I couldn't yet see how a concern of that sort should have anything to do with one's spiritual life. To me, religion ought to have been a matter of good men praying alone and meeting by twos and threes to talk of spiritual matters. And then the fussy, time-wasting botheration of it all! the bells, the crowds, the umbrellas, the notices, the bustle, the perpetual arranging and organising. Hymns were (and are) extremely disagreeable to me. Of all musical instruments I liked (and like) the organ least. I have, too, a sort of spiritual *gaucherie* which makes me unapt to participate in any rite.

Thus my churchgoing was a merely symbolical and provisional practice. If it in fact helped to move me in the Christian direction, I was and am unaware of this. My chief companion on this stage of the road was Griffiths, with whom I kept up a copious correspondence. Both now believed in God, and were ready to hear more of Him from any source, Pagan or Christian. In my mind (I cannot now answer for his, and he has told his own story admirably in *The Golden String*) the perplexing multiplicity of 'religions' began to sort itself out. The real clue had been put into my hand by that hard-boiled Atheist when he said, 'Rum thing, all that about the Dying God. Seems to have really happened once'; by him and by Barfield's encouragement of a more respectful, if not more delighted, attitude to Pagan myth. The question was no longer to find the one simply true religion among a thousand religions simply false. It was rather, 'Where has religion reached its true maturity? Where, if anywhere, have the hints of all Paganism been fulfilled?' With the irreligious I was no longer concerned; their view of life was henceforth out of court. As against them, the whole mass of those who had worshipped—all who had danced and sung and sacrificed and trembled and adored—were clearly right. But the intellect and the conscience, as well as the orgy and the ritual, must be our guide. There could be no question of going back to primitive, untheologised and unmoralised, Paganism. The God whom I had at last acknowledged was one, and was righteous. Paganism had been only the childhood of religion, or only a prophetic dream. Where was the thing full grown? or where was the awaking? (*The Everlasting Man* was helping me here.) There were really only two answers possible: either in Hinduism or in Christianity. Everything else was either a preparation for, or else (in the French sense) a *vulgarisation* of, these. Whatever you could find elsewhere you could find better in one of these. But Hinduism seemed to have two disqualifications. For one thing, it appeared to be not so much a moralised and philosophical maturity of Paganism as a mere oil-and-water coexistence of philosophy side by side with Paganism unpurged; the Brahmin meditating in the forest, and, in the village a few miles away, temple prostitution, *sati,* cruelty, monstrosity. And secondly, there was no such historical claim as in Christianity. I was by now too experienced in literary criticism to regard the Gospels as myths. They had not the mythical taste. And yet the very matter which they set down in their artless, historical fashion—those narrow, unattractive Jews, too blind to the mythical wealth of the Pagan world around them—was precisely the matter of the great myths. If ever a myth had become fact, had been incarnated, it would be just like this. And nothing else in all literature was just like this. Myths were like it in one way. Histories were like it in another. But nothing was simply like it. And no person was like the Person it depicted; as real, as recognisable, through all that depth of time, as Plato's Socrates or Boswell's Johnson (ten times more so than Eckermann's Goethe or Lockhart's Scott), yet also numinous, lit by a light from beyond the world, a god. But if a god—we are no longer polytheists—then not a god, but God. Here and here only in all time the myth must have become fact; the Word, flesh; God, Man. This is not 'a religion', nor 'a philosophy'. It is the summing up and actuality of them all.

As I have said, I speak of this last transition less certainly than of any which went before it, and it may be that in the preceding paragraph I have mixed thoughts that came later. But I can hardly be wrong about the main lines. Of one thing I am sure. As I drew near the conclusion, I felt a resistance almost as strong as my previous resistance to Theism. As strong, but shorter-lived, for I understood it better. Every step I had taken, from the Absolute to 'Spirit' and from 'Spirit' to 'God', had been a step towards the more concrete, the more imminent, the more compulsive. At each step one had less chance 'to call one's soul one's own'. To accept the Incarnation was a further step in the same direction. It brings God nearer, or near in a new way. And this, I found, was something I had not wanted. But to recognise the ground for my evasion was of course to recognise both its shame and its futility. I know very well when, but hardly how, the final step was taken. I was driven to Whipsnade one sunny morning. When we set out I did not believe that Jesus Christ is the Son of God, and when we reached the zoo I did. Yet I had not exactly spent the journey in thought. Nor in great emotion. *Emotional* is perhaps the last word we can apply to some of the most important events. It was more like when a man, after long sleep, still lying motionless in bed, becomes aware that he is now awake. And it was, like that moment on top of the bus, ambiguous. Freedom, or necessity? Or do they differ at their maximum? At that maximum a man is what he does; there is nothing of him left over or outside the act. As for what we commonly call Will, and what we commonly call Emotion, I fancy these usually talk too loud, protest too much, to be quite believed, and we have a secret suspicion that the great passion or the iron resolution is partly a put-up job.

They have spoiled Whipsnade since then. Wallaby Wood, with the birds singing overhead and the bluebells underfoot and the Wallabies hopping all round one, was almost Eden come again.

But what, in conclusion, of Joy? For that, after all, is what the story has mainly been about. To tell you the truth, the subject has lost nearly all interest for me since

I became a Christian. I cannot, indeed, complain, like Wordsworth, that the visionary gleam has passed away. I believe (if the thing were at all worth recording) that the old stab, the old bitter-sweet, has come to me as often and as sharply since my conversion as at any time of my life whatever. But I now know that the experience, considered as a state of my own mind, had never had the kind of importance I once gave it. It was valuable only as a pointer to something other and outer. While that other was in doubt, the pointer naturally loomed large in my thoughts. When we are lost in the woods the sight of a signpost is a great matter. He who first sees it cries 'Look!' The whole party gathers round and stares. But when we have found the road and are passing signposts every few miles, we shall not stop and stare. They will encourage us and we shall be grateful to the authority that set them up. But we shall not stop and stare, or not much; not on this road, though their pillars are of silver and their lettering of gold. 'We would be at Jerusalem.'

Not, of course, that I don't often catch myself stopping to stare at roadside objects of even less importance.